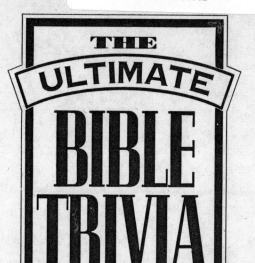

BOB PHILLIPS

HARVEST HOUSE PUBLISHERS
Eugene, Oregon 97402

THE ULTIMATE BIBLE TRIVIA CHALLENGE
formerly *In Search of Bible Trivia*, Volumes 1 & 2

Copyright © 1992 by Harvest House Publishers
Eugene, Oregon 97402

Library of Congress Catalog Card Number 92-90542
ISBN 1-56507-020-8

Dedication

*To my wife Pam
and my daughters, Lisa and Christy,
and to all who enjoy the little-known facts
of the Bible.*

OTHER BOOKS
BY BOB PHILLIPS

LAST OF THE GOOD CLEAN JOKES
by *Bob Phillips*

The master joker edits and arranges wisecracks, rib ticklers, and zany puns.

MORE GOOD CLEAN JOKES
by *Bob Phillips*

An entertaining fun-book designed for public speakers, pastors, and everyone who enjoys good clean jokes.

THE RETURN OF THE GOOD CLEAN JOKES
by *Bob Phillips*

Over 900 quips, anecdotes, gags, puns, and wisecracks. An ideal resource for pastors and speakers, as well as wonderful fun for family and enemies.

THE WORLD'S GREATEST COLLECTION OF CLEAN JOKES
by *Bob Phillips*

For everyone who enjoys wholesome humor. This collection of 1000 jokes has already sold over 250,000 copies.

GOOD CLEAN JOKES FOR KIDS
by *Bob Phillips*

Tongue-twisters...riddles...knock-knock jokes. All these and more come to life in this collection guaranteed to inspire smiles, laughter, and even a few groans. These rib-ticklers are just the thing for family trips or any time kids want to have fun.

CONTENTS

INTRODUCTION

For a number of years I have collected unusual Bible facts, Bible puns, and riddles to share with friends and to add a little sparkle to sermons. The renewed interest in various kinds of trivia prompted me to compile this fun collection of well-known and little-known Bible facts. Also included is a section on humorous Bible puns and riddles.

The Ultimate Bible Trivia Challenge can be utilized in a number of different ways:

- You can read it just for your own personal amusement and review of your Bible knowledge. It is designed in such a way that you can write down your answers to the questions.

- You can use the unusual facts to add interest and humor to your public speaking.

- You can use the book as a tool to help pass the time while traveling as a family. Many of the facts will spark discussion about Bible events and stories.

- You can utilize the little-known facts as an icebreaker at various get-togethers.

- You can take various questions in the book and use them as part of a Biblical pursuit game with a small group of friends.

- You can share the questions on a large group or team basis also. Questions along with the answers are repeated in the back of the book. This was done in the event you would like to ask questions of a group and have an immediate answer ready. You will find a large group game like this to be much fun for everyone.

As you read *The Ultimate Bible Trivia Challenge*, I hope you will have as much fun answering the questions as I did in compiling them.

—Bob Phillips
Hume, California

EASY TRIVIA QUESTIONS

1. How many men did Nebuchadnezzar see walking in the fiery furnace?

   _____

2. What did Noah see in the sky?

   _____

3. "For whatsoever a man soweth, _____

   _____."

4. "But _____ found grace in the eyes of the Lord."

5. "Delilah said to _____, Tell me, I pray thee, wherein thy great strength lieth."

6. "Pride goeth before destruction, and a haughty spirit

   before _____."

7. "Follow me and I will make you _____."

8. "Come unto me, all ye that labor and are _____."

9. What were the names of the three disciples who were on the Mount of Transfiguration with Jesus?

_____

10. What was the name of the village that was known as the "City of David"?

_____

11. Who was Andrew's brother?

_____

12. "A soft answer turneth away _____."

13. The disciples were told to be wise as _____ and

harmless as _____.

14. In what city did Joseph, Mary, and Jesus live?

_____

15. What country did Joseph, Mary, and Jesus flee to?

_____

16. Where did the Wise Men come from?

_____

17. In the parable of the ten virgins, how many were wise and how many were foolish?

_____

18. Where did Jesus perform His first miracle?

_____

19. John the Baptist had an interesting diet of what?

_____

20. In what book of the Bible do you find these words? "I am the living bread which came down from heaven; if any man eat of this bread, he shall live for ever."

_____

21. Peter said to Jesus, "Thou shalt never wash _____."
    a. My hands   b. My feet   c. My hair
    d. My clothes   e. My cup

22. Who prayed three times a day at an open window?

_____

23. Who had an occupation as a tentmaker?

_____

24. Jesus was arrested in _____.

25. Who in the Bible could be called "The Lion Tamer"?

_____

26. John the Baptist was how much older than Jesus?

_____

27. Who in the Bible could carry the title "The Strong Man"?

_____

28. "If God be for us, _____

_____?"

29. In what book of the Bible do you find the words, "There is no new thing under the sun"?

_____

30. According to the book of Proverbs, the beginning of

knowledge is _____.

31. Who was the man who said, "Every kind of beasts, and of birds hath been tamed by mankind"?

_____

32. In what book of the Bible do you find the story of the burning bush?

_____

33. To whom did Jesus say, "Get thee behind me, Satan"?

_____

34. Who prayed inside of a fish?

_____

35. What is the longest psalm in the Bible?

_____

36. The wise man built his house on _____ and the

foolish man built his house on _____.

37. What was the name of the special food that God provided for the children of Israel during the forty years in
the wilderness?

_____

38. "I am _____ and _____, the beginning and the
ending."

39. In what book of the Bible do you find the following
words? "And there are also many other things which
Jesus did, the which, if they should be written every one,
I suppose that even the world itself could not contain the
books that should be written."

_____

40. Who in the Bible could carry the title "The Wise King"?

_____

41. Bartimaeus was:

a. Lame   b. Deaf   c. Blind   d. Leprous

42. Who owned a coat that had many colors?

_____

43. "I am the true _____, and my Father is the husband-man."

44. What Bible character was turned into a pillar of salt?

    _____

45. What Bible character ate food that was given to the pigs?

    _____

46. What type of animal did Aaron fashion out of gold?

    _____

47. In what book in the Bible do you find the following words? "In my Father's house are many mansions."

    _____

48. Who wrote with His finger on the ground?

    _____

49. Name the three gifts that the Wise Men from the East brought to Baby Jesus.

    _____

50. "For what shall it profit a man, if he shall gain _____

    _____?"

51. How many books are in the New Testament?
    a. 23   b. 25   c. 27   d. 29

52. "Pray without _____ "

53. Where in the Bible do you find the following words? "Behold, I stand at the door, and knock."

   _____

54. Who said, "Silver or gold have I none, but such as I have give I thee"?

   _____

55. What is the first lie to be recorded in the Bible?

   _____

56. "I can do all things through _____."

57. How many books are in the Old Testament?
   a. 33   b. 35   b. 37   d. 39

58. The book of Hebrews tells us to entertain strangers

   because they might be _____.

59. "Let the word of Christ dwell in you _____."

60. "Whatsoever ye do in word or deed, do all _____

   _____ "

61. "The _____ of a good man are ordered by the Lord."

62. "I am the good _____."

63. "Be not overcome of evil, but _____
_____."

64. "I am the _____ of the _____."

65. "I am the _____, the _____, and the _____."

66. "I am the _____; by me if any man enter in, he shall be saved."

67. "If thy right eye offend thee, _____."

68. Who in the Bible was called, "A man after mine own heart"?

_____

69. Who said, "Every son that is born ye shall cast into the river, and every daughter ye shall save alive"?

_____

70. To whom was the following said? "Loose thy shoe from off thy foot; for the place whereon thou standest is holy."

_____

71. "_____, and it shall be given you; _____, and ye shall find: _____, and it will be opened unto you."

72. Who said, "When I was a child, I spake as a child, I understood as a child, I thought as a child"?

_____

73. Who said, "How can a man be born when he is old"?

_____

74. "For the wages of sin is death; _____

_____."

75. Who said, "By their fruits ye shall know them"?

_____

76. Who said, "Almost thou persuadest me to be a Christian"?

_____

77. In what book in the Bible do you find the following? "So Joseph died, being a hundred and ten years old."

_____

78. Who said, "Who touched my clothes?"

_____

79. To whom was the following spoken? "He was a murderer from the beginning, and abode not in the truth, because there is no truth in him."

_____

80. What was the name of Abraham's wife?

_____

81. In what book of the Bible do you find the laws concerning the eating of clean things?

_____

82. In what book of the Bible do you find the phrase, "God is love"?

_____

83. "Thy word is a lamp unto my feet, and _____

_____."

84. "For many are called, _____."

85. What is the shortest verse in the New Testament?

_____

86. "O death, where is thy sting? _____

_____?"

87. How did Judas indicate to the crowd who Jesus was?

_____

88. Who in the Bible could be called "Mr. Patience"?

_____

89. To whom were the following words spoken? "Because thou has done this, thou are cursed."

_____

90. David's occupation before he became a king was _____
    _____.

91. "And ye shall know the truth, and the truth shall _____
    _____."

92. What is greater than faith and hope?

    _____

93. What happens when the blind lead the blind?

    _____

94. To whom was the following comment made? "For God so loved the world, that he gave his only begotten Son, that whosoever believeth in him should not perish, but have everlasting life."

    _____

95. "For where two or three are gathered together in my

    name, _____."

96. In what book of the Bible do you find the following words? "Let everything that hath breath praise the Lord."

    _____

97. Cain did what for a living?

    _____

98. Peter did what for a living?

_____

99. Which apostle was called Doubting _____?

100. Abel did what for a living?

_____

101. Joseph, the husband of Mary, did what for a living?

_____

102. In what book of the Bible do you find the words, "Blessed is the man that walketh not in the counsel of the ungodly"?

_____

103. "Speak; for thy servant _____."

104. In what book of the Bible do you find the words, "in the beginning was the Word and the Word was with God, and the Word was God"?

_____

105. "The Lord is my strength and _____ "

106. Who said that even all the hairs on our head are numbered by God?

_____

107. Paul told Timothy to take something for his stomach's sake. What was it?

_____

108. "Greater love hath no man than this, _____

_____."

109. When did Jesus make more than a hundred gallons of very good wine?

_____

110. Who made clothes out of leaves that were sewed together?

_____

111. Who was the wife of Boaz?

_____

112. Who in the Bible could be called "The Giant Killer"?

_____

113. Who was the oldest brother—Cain or Abel?

_____

114. Who gave Jesus some food to help feed the 5000?

_____

115. Who said, "My soul doth magnify the Lord...he hath

regarded the low estate of his handmaiden...generations shall call me blessed"?

116. Who said that, "I have fought a good fight, I have finished my course, I have kept the faith"?

117. What was the name of the man who gave each man in his army of 300 a trumpet and an empty pitcher?

118. Who took golden earrings and made them into a calf?

119. Jesus said, "Peace, be still." Who was He addressing?

120. "Saul hath slain his thousands, and David his _____

_____."

121. What was Paul's other name?

122. Jesus mixed something with clay and put it on the eyes of the blind man to make him see. What did Jesus mix with the clay?

123. When the Roman soldiers pierced Jesus in the side with a spear, what came out?

_____

124. "For what is a man profited, if he shall gain the whole world, and lose his own _____."

125. Did Judas Iscariot keep the betrayal money or did he give it back?

_____

126. The Spirit of God descended on Jesus in the form of a

_____.

127. "For the law was given by Moses, but grace and _____ came by Jesus Christ."

128. What did Ananias sell in order to get money to give to the apostles?

_____

129. Who said, "No prophet is accepted in his own country"?

_____

130. Water was in how many pots that Jesus turned into wine?

_____

131. Who was Jesus talking about when he said, "I have not found so great a faith, no, not in Israel"?

_____

132. "Go ye therefore, and teach all nations, baptizing them

_____."

133. "Judge not, _____."

134. Who brought back to life the son of the widow in whose house he was staying?

_____

135. What was the name of the garden Jesus prayed in?

_____

136. In what book of the Bible do we read about God's armor?

_____

137. "Without the _____ _____ _____ there is no forgiveness" (NIV).

138. How many demons did Mary Magdalene have in her?

    a. Two   b. Three   c. Five   d. Seven   e. Nine

139. How old was the daughter of Jairus?

_____

140. What book comes before 1 Kings?

_____

141. What are the names of the two men who had a sharp argument over John Mark?

_____

142. Which chapter in the Bible lists the heroes of faith?

_____

143. What Bible character stood on Mars Hill?

_____

144. "With God all things are _____."

145. A man who has his quiver full of them is happy. What is in the quiver?

_____

146. Who was the first person to experience fear in the Bible?

_____

147. "_____ _____ is the same yesterday and today and forever" (NIV).

148. Peter says that in the last days _____ will come.

149. Who shut the door on Noah's Ark?

_____

150. What time of day did Adam and Eve hear God walking in the Garden of Eden?

_____

151. Who said, "I will exalt my throne above the stars of God"?

_____

152. What Bible character talks about "the twinkling of an eye"?

_____

153. Who was the first person in the Bible to take a nap?

_____

154. Paul prayed _____ times to have his thorn in the flesh removed.

155. Quote Romans 3:23.

_____

156. What Bible character said, "Where your treasure is, there will your heart be also"?

_____

157. What is the book just before Micah?

_____

158. Into how many pieces was Jesus' seamless garment cut?

_____

159. In what book of the Bible does it talk about 100-pound (or a talent) hailstones?

_____

160. Who had a spear with the iron head weighing 600 shekels?

_____

161. In what chapter of the Bible do we find Jesus' high priestly prayer?

_____

162. The Egyptians thought Sarah was related to Abraham in what way?

_____

163. Which tribe of Israel had the responsibility of moving the tabernacle?

_____

164. What book comes after the book of Obadiah?

_____

165. What is the first word in the Bible?

_____

166. In what chapter of the Bible do you find the phrase, "He leadeth me beside the still waters"?

_____

167. God told Adam and Eve not to eat what kind of fruit?

_____

168. "_____ goeth before destruction, and a haughty spirit before a fall."

169. When Jesus was 12 He was unintentionally left behind by Mary and Joseph. How many days did they look for Him?

_____

170. How many times a year did the high priest enter the Holy of Holies to make atonement for all the sins of Israel?

_____

171. Who said, "Naked I came from my mother's womb" (NIV).

_____

172. How old was Jesus when it was first mentioned that He went to Jerusalem for the Passover?

_____

173. How many men believed in Christ after Peter's second sermon?

_____

174. "For the wages of sin is _____, but the gift of God is

    _____ _____" (NIV).

175. Two Old Testament cities were destroyed because of their great wickedness. What were their names?

    _____

176. In the Garden of Gethsemane, Jesus sweat great drops

    of _____.

177. The Bible suggests that a thousand years in God's sight is as how long?

    _____

178. Who said, "Foxes have holes and birds of the air have nests" (NIV)?

    _____

179. Which of the 12 disciples was in charge of the money?

    _____

180. What book comes before the book of Lamentations?

    _____

181. Who said, "Before Abraham was born, I am" (NIV)?

    _____

182. In what book of the Bible do we find the quotation, "God helps those who help themselves"?

_____

183. What is the name of the disciple who took care of Jesus' mother after His death?

_____

184. Quote Philippians 4:4.

_____

185. What book comes before the book of Isaiah?

_____

186. What Bible character said, "What must I do to be saved?"

_____

187. How many chapters are there in the book of Jude?

_____

188. Who asked Jesus, "Are you the king of the Jews?" (NIV).

_____

189. "Trust in the Lord with all thine _____: and lean

not unto thine own _____."

190. When the Philistines finally captured Samson, what did they do to him?

_____

191. What was the first thing that Adam and Eve did after they sinned?

_____

192. "For nothing is _____ with God" (NIV).

193. What are the names of the two Bible characters who did not die?

_____

194. "For by grace are ye _____ through _____; and that not of yourselves: it is the gift of God."

195. Peter suggests that the day of the Lord will come as a

_____.

196. What Bible character said, "I am a man of unclean lips"?

_____

197. What chapter of the Bible is considered the love chapter?

_____

198. "The _____ says in his heart, 'There is no
     _____.'" (NIV).

199. On the seventh day of creation, what did God do?

     _____

200. Who told the first lie in the Bible?

     _____

201. When Jesus healed the ten lepers, how many returned
     and thanked Him?

     _____

202. How many days did it take Nehemiah to inspect the
     city walls of Jerusalem before rebuilding them?

     _____

203. Quote John 1:12.

     _____

204. What was the hometown of King David?

     _____

205. What book comes after the book of Malachi?

     _____

206. John wrote the book of Revelation on what island?

     _____

207. How many chapters are there in the book of Colossians?

_____

208. In what book of the Bible do we find the words, "Abstain from all appearance of evil"?

_____

209. On what mountain did Noah's Ark come to rest?

_____

210. What are the names of the two men who wrapped Jesus' body for burial?

_____

211. The poor widow in the book of Luke put how many coins into the temple treasury?

_____

212. In what book of the Bible do we find the phrase, "The very hairs of your head are all numbered"?

_____

213. Who is the author of the book of Zephaniah?

_____

214. Who was the first person to enter the empty tomb of Jesus?

_____

215. Isaiah compares our righteousness to _____ _____.

216. What is the number of the beast in the book of Revelation?

217. In what book of the Bible do we find the phrase, "Give us this day our daily bread"?

218. Who succeeded Moses as leader of the children of Israel?

219. In what book of the Bible do we find the words, "Without the shedding of blood there is no forgiveness"?

220. Who disguises himself as an angel of light?

221. When David was a boy, what two fierce animals did he kill?

222. How many years will Satan be bound in the Abyss (bottomless pit)?

223. What was the name of the type of leaf that Adam and Eve wore before the fall?

_____

224. What Bible character originally said, "It is more blessed to give than to receive" (NIV)?

_____

225. Name the first five people mentioned in the Bible.

_____

226. How many of the sacrifice sheep did Moses take into the Ark with him?

_____

227. Lydia is known for selling what?

_____

228. What does the Bible say has never been tamed by man?

_____

229. The Bible says there is one thing that never fails. What is it?

_____

230. In what book of the Bible do we find the words, "For my yoke is easy and my burden is light"?

_____

231. How many times is the word Bible used in the Bible?

_____

232. What book comes after the book of Micah?

_____

233. "For where your _____ is, there your _____

will be also" (NIV).

234. What book comes after the book of Hebrews?

_____

235. On what two parts of the body will the mark of the beast be placed?

_____

236. In what book of the Bible do you find the words born again?

_____

237. In what book of the Bible is the verse, "Cleanliness is next to godliness"?

_____

238. Jonah purchased his boat ticket in what city?

_____

239. "I can do all things through _____ who _____ me."

240. What are the names of the three disciples who were the shortest distance from Jesus in Gethsemane while He prayed?

_____

241. In what book of the Bible do we find the words, "If any of you lack wisdom, let him ask of God"?

_____

242. What is the name of the disciple who was instructed to touch the nail prints in Jesus' hands after His resurrection?

_____

243. What was the name of the angel who spoke to Mary the mother of Jesus?

_____

244. Judas agreed to betray for how many pieces of silver?

_____

245. What Bible character said, "How can a man be born when he is old?"

_____

246. Who does the Bible say holds the keys of hell and death?

_____

247. What were the names of the two sisters of Lazarus?

_____

248. What kind of valley is described in Psalm 23?

_____

249. What Bible character put out a fleece to test God?

_____

FAIRLY EASY TRIVIA QUESTIONS

1. What was the name of the prophet who was very hairy and wore a leather belt?

   _____

2. What is the name of the man who King David arranged to have killed because he wanted his wife?

   _____

3. The earth, seas, grass, herb yielding seed, and the tree yielding fruit were created on which day of creation?

   a. 2nd   b. 3rd   c. 4th   d. 5th

4. What was the name of the man who inherited Elijah's mantle?

   _____

5. What was the name of the man who owned a seamless coat?

   _____

6. What was the name of a man who worked seven years to earn a wife?

   _____

7. What Bible prophet said, "Behold, a virgin shall conceive, and bear a son, and shall call his name Immanuel"?

   _____

8. How old was Joseph when he was given his coat of many colors?

   _____

9. What was the name of the high priest's servant who had his ear cut off by the Apostle Peter?

   _____

10. What was the name of the Bible character who was blind and killed 3000 people while at a religious feast?

    _____

11. What was the name of the Jewish man who called himself greater than King Solomon?

    _____

12. After David knocked Goliath to the ground with a stone from his sling, he cut off Goliath's head with his own sword. True or false?

    _____

13. What nation of people got sick and tired of eating quail for dinner?

_____

14. Which came first—the plague of lice or the plague of frogs?

_____

15. What was the name of the Bible prophet who was fed by birds?

_____

16. About whom was the following statement made? "Among those that are born of women there is not a greater prophet than…"?

_____

17. On what mountain did Noah's Ark come to rest?

_____

18. What was the name of the queen who came from a far country to witness for herself the wisdom of King Solomon?

_____

19. What was the name of the man who wore clothes made out of camel's hair?

_____

20. At whose command were 300 pitchers broken?

_____

21. How many days was Saul blind while in Damascus?

_____

22. Who were the people who found frogs on their beds and in their ovens?

_____

23. Who said, "Divide the living child in two, and give half to the one, and half to the other"?

_____

24. What was the name of the Bible character who was a cupbearer to a king and also an engineer?

_____

25. What was the name of the man who came to Jesus by night to talk with him?

_____

26. How old was Methuselah when he died?

_____

27. Name the fruit of the Spirit.

_____

28. How many windows were in Noah's Ark?

_____

29. What was the name of the man who was released from prison by an angel?

_____

30. In what book of the Bible do you find the words, "Of making many books there is no end"?

_____

31. What were the names of the two disciples who were called "The Sons of Thunder"?

_____

32. In order to see Jesus more clearly, Zacchaeus climbed what type of tree?

_____

33. What was the name of the man who escaped from Damascus in a basket?

_____

34. How many people were saved in Noah's Ark?

_____

35. What was the name of the man who issued the decree that all the world should be taxed?

_____

36. What was the name of the tree that Adam and Eve were told not to eat fruit from?

_____

37. What was the name of the man who foretold of the seven good years and the seven lean years in Egypt?

_____

38. What was the name of the first woman judge in Israel?

_____

39. What was the name of the couple who died because they lied to the Holy Spirit?

_____

40. Who was accused of eating in the cornfields on the Sabbath?

_____

41. The Israelites were bitten by _____ and were healed by looking at the same creature made out of brass.

42. Moses had a brother. What was his name?

_____

43. How many times did Samuel go to Eli the priest, thinking that Eli had called him?

_____

44. What was the name of the queen who was devoured by dogs?

_____

45. How old was Joseph when his brothers sold him into slavery?

_____

46. What is the name of the angel who told Mary that she would be the mother of Jesus?

_____

47. How many years did the children of Israel eat manna?

_____

48. How many years did God give Noah to build the Ark?

_____

49. How many stories or levels were in the Ark?

_____

50. What was the name of the father who was struck dumb, because of unbelief, until his son was born?

_____

51. What was the name of the man who had to work many years and got two wives as a result?

_____

52. What was in the Ark in the Tabernacle?

_____

53. The Bible talks of a very tiny seed that becomes a very large tree. What is the name of the seed?

_____

54. How many Marys are mentioned in the Bible?

_____

55. What was the name of the woman who was called "The Seller of Purple"?

_____

56. What is the last line of the Twenty-third Psalm?

_____

57. Jesus said that He would rebuild the temple in how many days?

_____

58. The manger is to Jesus as the basket in the bulrushes is to _____.

59. Who said, "Repent ye: for the kingdom of heaven is at hand"?

_____

60. On what mountain did Moses receive the law?

_____

61. Who replaced Moses as the leader of the children of Israel?

_____

62. To whom was the following statement made? "Take nothing for your journey, neither staves, nor scrip, neither bread, neither money; neither have two coats apiece."

_____

63. Timotheus' mother was a Jewess and his father was

_____.

64. What color was Esau's complexion?

   a. Pale   b. Light brown   c. Red
   d. Black   e. White

65. What color was the robe that Jesus wore when the soldiers taunted Him?

_____

66. Genesis is to Malachi as Matthew is to _____.

67. Matthew, Mark, and John called it Golgotha or the place of the skull. What did Luke call it?

_____

68. In what book of the Bible do you find the words, "Make haste, my beloved, and be thou like to a roe or to a young hart upon the mountains of spices"?

69. In what book of the Bible do you find the words, "Be strong and of a good courage"?

    a. Job   b. Philippians   c. Joshua
    d. Ephesians

70. Who said, "I am innocent of the blood of this just person"?

71. How many hours was Jesus on the cross?

72. What was the relationship of Zebedee to James and John?

73. In what book of the Bible do you find the words, "Blessed are the meek: for they shall inherit the earth"?

74. In what book of the Bible do you find the Ten Commandments?

75. Who said, "He was oppressed, and he was afflicted, yet he opened not his mouth"?

   a. Isaiah   b. Jeremiah   c. Ezekiel   d. Hosea

76. Who was born first—Jacob or Esau?

   _____

77. The spies who spied out the land of Canaan said that it

   flowed with _____ and _____.

78. Who was stoned to death for preaching that Jesus was the savior?

   _____

79. "It is easier for a _____ to go through the eye of a

   _____, than for a _____ to enter into the kingdom of God."

80. In the parable of the ten virgins, five of them were wise and five were foolish. Why were the foolish ones foolish?

   _____

81. Who were the disciples who argued about sitting on the right and left hand side of Jesus?

   _____

82. Who witnessed the conversation between Moses, Elijah, and Jesus?

   _____

83. On what day of creation were the sun, the moon, and the stars created?

   _____

84. Paul and Barnabas had an argument over a certain man traveling with them on their missionary journey. What was the man's name?

   _____

85. What were the names of the two spies who spied Canaan Land and gave a favorable report?

   _____

86. What Bible character was renamed Israel?

   _____

87. What preacher was mad because his preaching caused a whole city to repent?

   _____

88. On what day of creation were the sea creatures and fowl created?

   _____

89. Who saw Satan fall from heaven?

   _____

90. Who had a wrestling match with God and won?

   _____

91. Which came first, "Thou shalt not kill" or "Thou shalt not steal"?

_____

92. What was the name of the apostle who was shipwrecked three different times?

_____

93. On which day of creation were the land animals and man created?

_____

94. What Bible character had 300 concubines?

_____

95. What was the name of a physician in the Bible who was also an author?

_____

96. Who sold their younger brother into slavery?

_____

97. Lot escaped from the city of Sodom with whom?

_____

98. What was the name of the man who ordered the execution of 450 priests?

_____

99. Which book in the Bible was written to an "Elect Lady"?

_____

100. Jesus said that it was proper to pay tribute (money) to what man?

_____

101. Simon Peter cut off the ear of the high priest's servant. Which ear did he cut off?

_____

102. What Bible character said, "A little leaven leaveneth the whole lump"?

_____

103. How many years did Jacob work for his Uncle Laban in payment for his daughters?

_____

104. Who was healed—the son or the daughter of Jairus?

_____

105. "Blessed are the pure in heart: _____

_____."

106. What book in the Bible has a threat against anyone adding to it or taking away from it?

_____

107. What was the name of the man who lifted up the infant Jesus at the temple and praised God?

_____

108. In what book in the Bible do you find the following: "For the Lord himself shall descend from heaven with a shout, with the voice of the archangel"?

_____

109. What sign was given to the shepherds at the time of Christ's birth?

_____

110. How many loaves and how many fishes did Jesus use to feed the 5000?

_____

111. For what reason did the rich young ruler come to Christ?

_____

112. What does the name Emmanuel mean?

_____

113. What was the name of the king who sought to take the life of the Baby Jesus?

_____

114. What was the name of the criminal who was released in place of Jesus?

_____

115. What was the name of the mother of Abraham's first son?

_____

116. What Bible character had a dream that his parents and brothers would bow down before him?

_____

117. The city walls of _____ fell down when the trumpets were blown.

118. Name the two bodies of water that the children of Israel crossed on dry ground.

_____

119. Where in the Bible do you find the longest recorded prayer of Jesus?

_____

120. What was Matthew's other name?

_____

121. What is the first beatitude?

_____

122. Is Bethlehem located in Galilee or in Judea?

_____

123. Jesus said that there were two masters you could not serve at the same time. What were they?

_____

124. What was Sarah's other name?

_____

125. Who said, "Am I my brother's keeper?"

_____

126. Who said, "The Lord gave, and the Lord hath taken away; blessed be the name of the Lord"?

_____

127. Who owned a coat that was dipped in blood?

_____

128. Who was bitten by a snake and shook it off into a fire and felt no harm?

_____

129. Peter was told by Jesus to forgive his brother how many times?

_____

130. Who was the first Bible character to use a riddle?

_____

131. What was the New Testament word for teacher?

_____

132. What is the name of the man who carried Jesus' cross?

_____

133. In order for a man to become a bond slave, what did he have to do?

_____

134. In speaking of Jesus, who said, "Certainly this was a righteous man"?

_____

135. How many men did Nebuchadnezzar see walking in the fiery furnace?

_____

136. In what book of the Bible do we read the words, "Whoso findeth a wife findeth a good thing"?

_____

137. What was the name of the Bible character who put a veil over his face to hide the glory of God?

_____

138. Jesus was a descendant of what tribe of Israel?

_____

139. Saul had a troubled spirit that could only be soothed by

_____.

140. The disciples were first called Christians in what city?

_____

141. What book comes before the book of Joel?

_____

142. Who prayed the shortest prayer recorded in the Bible?

_____

143. Quote the shortest prayer in the Bible.

_____

144. What Bible character said, "What a wretched man I am" (NIV).

_____

145. What man in the Bible was called the Son of Encouragement (or consolation)?

_____

146. Quote Isaiah 53:6.

_____

_____

147. In what book of the Bible do we read the words, "Your attitude should be the same as that of Christ Jesus" (NIV)?

_____

148. "Believe on the Lord Jesus Christ, and thou shalt be

_____, and thy _____."

149. In what book of the Bible do we read the words, "Whatsoever a man soweth, that shall he also reap"?

_____

150. What does Proverbs 22 suggest is more desirable than great riches?

_____

_____

151. What is the name of the first Bible character mentioned drinking wine?

_____

152. What is the number of the largest group of people to whom Christ appeared after His resurrection?

_____

153. Name the three Bible characters who are mentioned as fasting for 40 days.

_____

154. List the books of the Bible that are named after women.

_____

155. Quote Philippians 1:21.

_____

156. If a man hates his son, he will not bother to do what?

_____

157. Which book comes before the book of Obadiah?

_____

158. What Bible character said, "Here am I; send me"?

_____

159. The country of Lebanon is famous for what kind of trees?

_____

160. _____ was called God's friend.

161. According to Timothy, what will people love in the last days?

_____

162. At the time of Christ's birth, who issued a decree for a census (NIV) or tax (KJV)?

_____

163. In what book of the Bible do we find the words, "Every man did that which was right in his own eyes"?

_____

164. What book comes after the book of Habakkuk?

_____

165. How many days after Jesus' resurrection did He ascend to heaven?

_____

166. What Bible character called her husband master (lord)?

_____

167. Name the Bible character who was buried by God.

_____

168. According to 2 Timothy, Scripture is profitable for four things. What are they?

_____

169. What was the name of the father of James and John?

_____

170. Did Hezekiah author the book of Hezekiah?

_____

171. Jesus told His disciples in the book of Acts that they would be witnesses in three specific locations. What were those locations?

_____

172. What did the rich man in hell want?

_____

173. Quote 1 Thessalonians 5:16.

_____

174. How did God punish Eve for sinning in the Garden of Eden?

_____

175. In the book of Romans, God is quoted as hating what Bible character?

_____

176. Ananias was told to go to a street called _____.

177. When Joshua entered the Promised Land, what was the name of the second city he attacked?

_____

178. Who was the first man to suggest that Jonah be thrown overboard as a result of the storm?

_____

179. What was the name of the Bible character who because of his age slept with a beautiful young virgin in order to keep warm?

_____

180. Which church in the book of Revelation was called lukewarm?

_____

181. When the Israelites complained about eating only manna, what did God do?

_____

182. Who was the prophet Samuel speaking to when he said, "To obey is better than sacrifice"?

_____

183. In the book of Acts, how many men were chosen to wait on tables?

_____

184. What is the name of the man who wanted to buy the ability to do miracles like Peter and John?

_____

185. Who were the first twins mentioned in the Bible?

_____

186. Quote Philippians 4:13.

_____

187. What was the name of Adam's son who replaced Abel?

_____

188. How did the prophet Elijah travel to heaven?

_____

189. Which two New Testament books instruct husbands to love their wives?

_____

190. After Dinah was raped by Shechem, what did her brothers do?

_____

191. In what book of the Bible do we find the words, "Though your sins are like scarlet, they shall be as white as snow" (NIV)?

_____

192. King Herod was eaten by _____.

193. In the Old Testament, murderers could flee to what cities in order to be safe?

_____

194. Which disciple objected to Mary washing Jesus' feet with perfume?

_____

195. What is the eighth book of the Bible?

_____

196. To whom was Paul speaking when he said, "Let no man despise thy youth"?

_____

197. What is the name of the Pharisee who defended the apostles before the Sanhedrin in the book of Acts?

_____

198. Who were the first Gentiles in Caesarea to be converted to Christianity?

_____

199. What is the name of the queen for whom the Ethiopian eunuch worked?

_____

200. Which is the longest book in the New Testament?

a. Matthew   b. Luke   c. Romans   d. Revelation

201. What is the name of the Bible character who said, "Let me inherit a double portion of your spirit" (NIV)?

_____

202. When Philip met the Ethiopian eunuch, he was reading from the book of which prophet?

_____

203. Quote 1 Thessalonians 5:18.

_____

204. In the book of Philemon, what is the name of the servant for whom Paul was making an appeal?

_____

205. What were the names of Job's three friends?

_____

206. As a result of Adam's sin, what became cursed?

_____

207. Who does James suggest will be judged more strictly than others?

_____

208. What is the name of the man whom King David made drunk?

_____

209. The book of Romans has how many chapters?

_____

210. Lydia, the seller of purple, was from which city?

_____

211. In what book of the Bible did Paul state that people who do not work should not eat?

_____

212. What New Testament book tells the story of a man eating a book (or scroll)?

_____

213. In what book of the Bible does it talk about Satan accusing believers before God day and night?

_____

214. In the book of Acts, what was the name of the man who predicted that a famine would spread over the entire Roman world?

_____

215. What does Proverbs say is a mocker? _____

216. The word Armageddon is used only one time in Scripture. In what book of the Bible is this word found?

_____

217. In what book in the Bible does it suggest that we not eat too much honey?

_____

218. In the book of Colossians there was a man named Justus. What was his famous other name?

_____

219. Who was the first person mentioned in the Bible as laughing?

_____

220. What does the Bible say was put in place to bring us to faith before Christ came?

_____

221. When David had to face Goliath, he picked up:

a. Three rough stones   b. Five smooth stones
c. Five rough stones   d. Three smooth stones

222. Which one of Noah's sons looked on Noah's nakedness?

_____

223. What is the name of the priest that Abram met in the valley of Shaveh?

_____

224. What is the name of the land that God told Abram to leave?

_____

225. In 1 Corinthians, what is the last enemy to be destroyed?

_____

226. Which of these did Jesus cure first?

a. Blindness   b. Leprosy   c. Lameness

227. What was the name of the man who made a metal snake and put it on a pole?

_____

228. In what book of the Bible do you find the words, "Remember your Creator in the days of your youth" (NIV)?

_____

229. Quote Romans 8:28.

_____

_____

_____

230. The book of Proverbs suggests that a good medicine is

a _____ _____.

231. When blind Bartimaeus came to Jesus, he threw something away. What was it?

_____

232. An Israelite man was exempt from war for how long after he was married?

_____

233. King Herod killed all the baby boys in Bethlehem who

were _____ years old and under.

234. What was the name of an angel that fought with the dragon in the book of Revelation?

_____

235. What was the name of Solomon's mother?

_____

236. What did the angels do to the homosexual men of Sodom to protect Lot?

_____

237. Why did Adam name his wife Eve?

_____

238. Who said, "I am slow of speech, and of a slow tongue"?

_____

239. What two things did God say would happen to Eve for disobedience in the Garden of Eden?

_____

240. Who said there is "a time to weep and a time to laugh"?

_____

241. In the book of Revelation, who held the key to the Abyss (bottomless pit)?

_____

242. Who said, "How beautiful are the feet of them that preach the gospel of peace"?

_____

243. Who wore golden bells on the hem of a blue robe?

_____

244. What was the name of the Bible character who had red hair like a garment all over his body?

_____

245. When Apollos came from Alexandria, he first preached in what city?

_____

246. In what New Testament book do you find the words, "What therefore God hath joined together let not man put asunder"?

_____

247. Philip had four daughters who had a special spiritual gift. What was that gift?

_____

248. What is the name of the only man mentioned in the Bible as being bald-headed?

_____

249. When the angel in the book of Revelation came to bind Satan, what two objects did he have in his hand?

_____

250. Jesus calls Himself the morning star in what book of the Bible?

_____

251. What Bible character describes his girlfriend's hair as a flock of goats descending from Gilead?

_____

252. After Jesus' trial, what color of robe was put on Him?

_____

253. Which book of the Bible says, "I would rather be a doorkeeper in the house of my God than dwell in the tents of the wicked" (NIV)?

_____

254. What is the thirtieth book of the Bible?

_____

255. Quote Philippians 4:19.

_____

_____

FAIRLY DIFFICULT TRIVIA QUESTIONS

1. Name the man who kept some of the spoils after the battle of Jericho and brought punishment to Israel.

   _____

2. How many of Jesus' brothers wrote books of the Bible?

   _____

3. What was the name of Hosea's wife?

   _____

4. What woman in the Bible tried to seduce a handsome slave?

   _____

5. What was the name of the king who made a speech and as a result was eaten by worms?

   _____

6. Miriam and Aaron were upset with Moses because he

   married a woman who was an _____

7. How many of the clean animals did Noah take into the Ark?

   _____

8. What was the name of a Bible character who told a riddle about a lion?

   _____

9. There was a very rich man who was a disciple of Jesus. What was his name?

   _____

10. What was the name of the queen who was thrown out of a window?

    _____

11. Solomon said that something "biteth like a serpent, stingeth like an adder." What was it?

    _____

12. What was the name of the city where King Ahasuerus lived?

    _____

13. David is to a sling as Samson is to _____

14. How many times did Noah send the dove from the Ark?

    _____

15. Who had shoes that lasted for forty years and did not wear out?

_____

16. What was the name of the father who had two daughters married to the same man?

_____

17. How many years were the Israelites in bondage as

slaves? _____

18. King Solomon had how many wives?

_____

19. Name the two men who entertained angels unaware.

_____

20. What was the name of the prophet who was swept away by a whirlwind?

_____

21. The Sabeans took his oxen and his donkeys, the lightning killed his sheep, the Chaldeans stole his camels, and his servants were killed. To whom did all these things happen?

_____

22. Who dreamed about a ladder which reached up to heaven?

_____

23. To whom were the following words addressed? "Get thee out of thy country, and from thy kindred, and from thy father's house, unto a land that I will shew thee."

_____

24. What Bible character was called "The Gloomy Prophet"?

_____

25. The man called Gehazi was a:

   a. Prophet   b. Servant   c. King
   d. Lawyer   e. Wicked priest

26. What is the name of the first of the twelve disciples to be murdered?

_____

27. David the shepherd was how old when he became King of Israel?

_____

28. Who owned dishes that were pure gold?

_____

29. Someone came to Pilate and begged for the body of the crucified Jesus. Who was he?

_____

30. In what book of the Bible do you find the following words? "For God shall bring every work into judgment,

with every secret thing, whether it be good, or whether it be evil."

_____

31. What was Lot's relationship with Abraham?

_____

32. What is the name of the town that is called "City of Palm Trees"?

_____

33. Shem is to Noah as David is to _____.

34. What was Jacob's relationship to Laban?

_____

35. What is the name of the first New Testament martyr?

_____

36. Name the pool that had five porches.

_____

37. Which came first—the Tower of Babel or the Flood?

_____

38. Lazarus is to Jesus as Eutychus is to _____.

39. There was a silversmith in Ephesus by the name of

_____.

40. What is the name of the Bible character that preached in a valley full of dead men's bones?

_____

41. How old was Joseph when Pharaoh made him a ruler?

_____

42. Apollos was a:

   a. King   b. God   c. Learned Jew
   d. Maker of tents

43. What was the name of the man who helped an African to understand the Scriptures?

_____

44. What Bible character used salt to purify drinking water?

_____

45. How old was Moses when he died?

_____

46. Something very special happened to a certain man when he was 600 years old. Who was he and what happened?

_____

47. How many times did the boy who Elisha raised from the dead sneeze?

_____

48. The Ark that Noah built was thirty cubits high, fifty cubits wide, and _____ cubits long.

49. Who said, "This day is this scripture fulfilled in your ears"?

_____

50. What Bible character ate a poor widow's last meal?

_____

51. In what book of the Bible does it describe hailstones weighing a talent each (about 100 pounds)?

_____

52. How many years did it take to build the temple in Jesus' time?

_____

53. Who was the man who ordered a cup to be put into a sack of corn?

_____

54. There are two orders of angels. Can you name them?

_____

55. Some angels came to speak with Lot. How many angels were there?

_____

56. How many psalms are there in the Old Testament?

_____

57. What is the name of the Bible character whose handkerchiefs were used to heal people?

_____

58. Joab was a:

   a. Scribe   b. Priest   c. King
   d. Soldier   e. Servant

59. What is the name of the man who was called "The
Supplanter"?

_____

60. What relationship was Mordecai to Esther?

_____

61. What is the name of the boy who was sent out into the
desert to die with his mother?

_____

62. What is the name of the man who offered thirty changes
of garments for solving a riddle?

_____

63. What was the name of a leper who was also the captain
of the host of the King of Syria?

_____

64. Who asked for the head of John the Baptist and got it?

_____

65. What are the three most famous heads of hair mentioned in the Bible?

_____

66. What was the name of the Egyptian who bought Joseph from the Midianites?

_____

67. One of Joseph's brothers said, "Let us not kill him." Who was that brother?

_____

68. Who could be called the great hunter of the Bible? (He also loved red meat.)

_____

69. The Gibeonites would have been killed by Joshua if it had not been for their old clothes, old shoes, and what kind of bread?

_____

70. When Joseph's brothers first came to Egypt, he put them into jail for:

a. 1 day   b. 2 days   c. 3 days   d. 4 days
e. 5 days   f. 6 days.

71. How many Herods are there in the Bible?

_____

72. What type of wood did Noah use when he built the Ark?

_____

73. How many elders did Moses appoint to help him share the load of dealing with the children of Israel?

_____

74. Who wrote the book of Lamentations?

_____

75. What three young men had a father who was 500 years old?

_____

76. There was a certain group of men who could not wear garments that would cause them to sweat. Who were these men?

_____

77. Abraham asked God to spare the city of Sodom if a certain number of righteous people lived there. What was the final figure that God said he would spare the city for?

_____

78. In whose tomb was Jesus buried?

_____

79. What was the name of the woman who cast her young son in the bushes to die?

_____

80. What was the name of the mother who hid her son in the bulrushes?

_____

81. Jesus cursed three cities. What were their names?

_____

82. What was the name of the country in which Jesus healed two demon-possessed individuals?

_____

83. How many loaves of bread did Jesus use in feeding the 4000?

_____

84. Abraham left what country?

_____

85. When Philip met the Ethiopian eunuch, he was reading from what book in the Old Testament?

_____

86. Paul preached on Mars Hill. In what city is Mars' Hill located?

_____

87. Into how many parts did the soldiers divide Jesus' garments?

88. What was the name of Jacob's firstborn child?

89. When Jacob followed Esau out of his mother's womb, he was holding onto what?

90. What happened to Jacob when he wrestled with God?

91. How many times did the children of Israel march around the city of Jericho?

    a. 2   b. 7   c. 13   d. 21   e. 49

92. What was the name of the wilderness in which John the Baptist preached?

93. What caused the large fish to vomit Jonah onto dry land?

94. Who cast down his rod before Pharaoh and the rod became a serpent?

95. Who said, "The dog is turned to his own vomit again"?

_____

96. "At midnight _____ and _____ prayed, and sang praises unto God; and the prisoners heard them."

97. God opened the mouth of a donkey and the donkey spoke to _____

98. What was the name of the centurion from Caesarea who was part of the Italian band?

_____

99. What was the name of Aquila's wife?

_____

100. What was the name of the man who carried the cross for Jesus?

_____

101. To whom was the following spoken? "Go near, and join thyself to this chariot."

_____

102. What was the name of Timothy's mother?

_____

103. Paul the Apostle was born in what city?

_____

104. What was the name of the prophet who foretold that Jesus would be born in Bethlehem?

_____

105. What relationship was Lois to Timothy?

_____

106. "As it is written, _____ have I loved, but _____ have I hated."

107. What is the name of the Old Testament prophet who foretold the virgin birth?

_____

108. To whom was the following spoken? "Silver and gold have I none; but such as I have give I thee: In the name of Jesus Christ of Nazareth rise up and walk."

_____

109. What is the name of the woman who hid two Israelite spies on the roof of her house?

_____

110. What Bible character saw a city coming down out of heaven?

_____

111. What is the name of the Bible character who went to visit the witch of Endor?

_____

112. A Christian who returns to a life of sin is likened to which animals?

_____

113. In what book of the Bible does it talk about blood running so deep that it reaches up to the bridles of horses?

_____

114. The furnace into which Shadrach, Meshach, and Abednego were tossed was heated how many times hotter than usual?

_____

115. How many times did Jacob bow as he approached Esau?

_____

116. What were the names of the two believers who discipled Apollos?

_____

117. What was the name of Mordecai's cousin whom he brought up?

_____

118. What is the name of the tree that stands on both sides of the river of the water of life in the book of Revelation?

_____

119. What is the name of the Bible character who got leprosy by sticking his hand inside his cloak?

120. Jesus said He could call on His Father for how many legions of angels?

121. What was the occupation of Jairus?

122. In what two books of the Bible do we find the phrase, "Be not weary in well doing"?

123. What was the first command the Bible mentions that God gave to Adam and Eve?

124. What was the name of the Bible character who was called "mighty in the Scriptures"?

125. The Year of Jubilee comes how often for the Israelites?

126. What will the gates of the holy city be made of?

127. How many bowls of water did Gideon squeeze out of his fleece?

_____

128. Satan smote Job with _____ from the soles of his feet to the top of his head.

129. Who suggested that it is not wise to spend too much time at your neighbor's house?

_____

130. What Bible character said, "Almost thou persuadest me to be a Christian"?

_____

131. David took two things from Saul while he was asleep. What were they?

_____

132. What is the name of the Bible character who took all of the gold articles out of Solomon's temple?

_____

133. In what book of the Bible do we read the words, "It is required in stewards that a man be found faithful"?

_____

134. Where did Job live?

    a. Puz   b. Buz   c. Uz   d. Luz   e. Zuz

135. What was the name of Elisha's servant?

_____

136. In what book of the Bible do we find the story about the sun standing still?

_____

137. Which men wanted to kill Lazarus?

_____

138. What color was manna?

    a. Yellowish b. Reddish   c. Brownish d. White

139. What two items that touched Paul were used then to heal people?

_____

140. In the Promised Land there were _____ cities of refuge.

141. Where does the Bible suggest that too much study is hard on the body?

_____

142. Ruth and Boaz had a son named _____.

143. In what book of the Bible do we find the words, "He who wins souls is wise" (NIV)?

_____

144. Zacchaeus repaid to the people he had cheated how many times the amount?

_____

145. Name the New Testament book that was written to Gaius.

_____

146. In what book of the Bible do we read the words, "For the love of money is the root of all evil"?

_____

147. The poles used in carrying the Ark of the Covenant were made out of what kind of wood?

_____

148. What was the other name of the Bible character called Didymus?

_____

149. Who is the judge and defender of widows?

_____

150. Does the Bible say that husbands should submit to their wives?

_____

151. Who said that the Jews had holes in their purses?

_____

152. Who is likened to a gold ring in a pig's snout?

_____

153. At what time of day did Eutychus go to sleep and fall

    out of the window? _____

154. In what book of the Bible do you find the words, "It is
    more blessed to give than to receive"?

_____

155. What two men were candidates for the position of the
    twelfth apostle after Judas' death?

_____

156. What is the name of the man who replaced Judas as the
    twelfth apostle?

_____

157. Earthly treasures are destroyed by three things. What
    are they?

_____

158. In what book of the Bible do you find the words, "Man
    looks at the outward appearance, but the Lord looks at
    the heart" (NIV)?

_____

159. According to Proverbs, the tongue of the wise brings
    what?

_____

160. At what time of day is it not good to loudly bless your neighbor?

_____

161. How many horns did the goat in Daniel's second vision have?

_____

162. What was the name of Moses' father?

_____

163. Who said, "But godliness with contentment is great gain"?

_____

164. In what book of the Bible are we told to cast our bread upon the waters?

_____

165. What was the name of the boy who was left under a bush to die?

_____

166. In order to be on the church widow's list, how old did a widow need to be?

_____

167. What was on each of the four corners of the bronze altar in the tabernacle?

_____

168. The book of 1 Chronicles spends most of its pages discussing which Bible character?

_____

169. King Og's bed was made of what kind of metal?
   a. Gold   b. Iron   c. Silver
   d. Steel   e. Brass

170. Paul asked Timothy to bring him two items while he was in prison. What were those items?

_____

171. What woman in the Bible faked a rape because she was mad?

_____

172. What was Tabitha's other name?

_____

173. What did Jesus and His disciples cross just before He was arrested?

_____

174. What does the Bible say cannot be bought for any price?

_____

175. The Bible says that male babies should be circumcised when they are how old?

_____

176. What is the name of the servant girl who answered the door when Peter escaped from prison?

_____

177. In the story of the rich man and Lazarus, how many brothers did the rich man have?

_____

178. How old was Isaac when he married Rebekah?

_____

179. When the kings of the East march westward, what river will dry up?

_____

180. What does "manna" mean?

_____

181. What are the names of the two women who fought over who would eat mandrakes?

_____

182. Where was the only place a Nazarite could cut his hair?

_____

183. The book of Proverbs names four things that are stately in their stride. What are they?

_____

184. In the book of Acts, Peter had a vision that repeated itself how many times?

_____

185. In the book of Revelation, what spice did the merchants of the earth sell to Babylon?

_____

186. Paul the apostle was stoned in what city?

_____

187. What is the name of the man who was ready to kill his son because he ate honey?

_____

188. What is the name of the man who was to provide for the needs of Mephibosheth?

_____

189. Manoah had a famous son. What was his name?

_____

190. When Abimelech set fire to the tower of Shechem, how many people died in the flames?

_____

191. Who does the Bible say goes around and whispers, peeps, and mutters?

_____

192. In what book of the Bible do we find mention of a mother eagle stirring up her nest?

_____

193. Who was the first person mentioned in the Bible as being put into prison?

_____

194. In which book of the Bible do we find mention of a synagogue of Satan?

_____

195. In the Old Testament, what particular people could not "make baldness upon their head" or cut off the edges of their beards?

_____

196. Who said that we should not curse rich people from our bedroom?

_____

197. How many times is the phrase "born again" mentioned in the Bible?

_____

198. How many times does the word trinity appear in the Bible?

_____

199. What Bible character fell on his face and laughed?

200. What Bible character said that laughter is mad (or foolish—NIV)?

201. Who said that even in laughter the heart is sorrowful (aches)?

202. In what book of the Bible does it say that, "A feast is made for laughter"?

203. What Bible character said, "Let your laughter be turned to mourning"?

204. What Bible character said, "The fear of the Lord, that is wisdom; and to depart from evil is understanding"?

205. What caused the flood waters to recede from the face of the earth?

206. How many years did Noah live after the flood?

207. What kind of grain did Boaz give to Ruth?

_____

208. In the book of Exodus, what was the color of the priest's robe?

_____

209. Saul was hiding in the _____ when he was to be presented as the king of Israel.

210. What was the name of Aaron's wife?

_____

211. Jesus was a high priest after the order of _____.

212. Paul and Silas prayed at what time of day while they were in jail?

_____

213. In what book of the Bible do you find the statement, "Thy navel is like a round goblet"?

_____

214. Who were called, "Liars, evil beasts, slow bellies"?

_____

215. In the book of Luke, who took away the key of knowledge?

_____

216. In what book of the Bible do we find the first mention of a holy kiss?

_____

217. Who sneezed seven times in the Bible?

_____

218. In which book of the Bible do we find the country of Spain mentioned?

_____

219. In what book of the Bible do we find mention of birthing stools?

_____

220. God said that anyone who would kill Cain would receive from Him _____ vengeance.

    a. Threefold   b. Sevenfold   c. Tenfold

221. What were the names of Noah's three daughters-in-law?

_____

222. What was the sign of the covenant between Abram and God?

_____

223. Who said, "Is anything too hard for the Lord?" (NIV)

_____

224. What did Lot offer to the men of the city of Sodom so they would not take the two angels?

_____

225. The division of angels called seraphs (seraphims—KJV) have how many wings?

_____

226. Who was called the king of righteousness in the book of Hebrews?

_____

227. In what book of the Bible does it talk about God giving names to all of the stars?

_____

228. Name the city in which Paul had his hair cut off because of a vow.

_____

229. On the sixth day the children of Israel were to gather how many omers of manna for each person?

_____

230. Who had the first navy mentioned in the Bible?

_____

231. To whom did Jesus say, "Thou gavest me no kiss"?

_____

232. In the book of Proverbs, the virtuous woman clothed her entire family in what color?

_____

233. What was the former name for the town of Bethel?

_____

234. The eighth plague that the Egyptians experienced was the plague of locusts. A strong wind carried the locusts away in which direction?

_____

HARD TRIVIA QUESTIONS

1. Who was hung on a gallows fifty cubits (about seventy-five feet) high?

   _____

2. What were the names of the first and last judges of Israel?

   _____

3. Who was the individual who watched over Baby Moses while he floated in the bulrushes?

   _____

4. What was the name of the mother who made a little coat for her son every year?

   _____

5. What Bible prophet spoke of the killing of the children?

   _____

6. What type of bird did Noah first send forth from the Ark?

   _____

7. The name of David's first wife was _____.

8. The title written above Jesus' cross said, "JESUS OF NAZARETH THE KING OF THE JEWS." Name the three languages that the title was written in.

_____

9. Because of Achan's sin he was stoned in the valley of

_____.

10. What was the name of the sorcerer who was struck blind by Paul the apostle?

_____

11. After Paul's shipwreck he swam to the island of _____.

12. What was the name of the wife of both Nabal and King David?

_____

13. Which of Joseph's brothers was left behind as a hostage when the other nine returned to bring Benjamin to Egypt?

_____

14. In order to win the battle with Amalek, Aaron and Hur

helped Moses by _____.

15. Zipporah had a very famous husband. What was his name?

_____

16. What was the name of the wife of Lapidoth and what is she famous for?

_____

17 When David scrabbled on the doors of the gate, and let spittle fall down on his beard, and pretended to be crazy, he was doing so because he was afraid of _____

18. In what book of the Bible do you find the following words: "As a jewel of gold in a swine's snout..."?

_____

19. What was Nebuchadnezzar's other name?

_____

20. "The Lord hath made all things for himself: yea, even the wicked for _____."

21. Hannah was the mother of Samuel. What was the name of Hannah's husband?

_____

22. To whom did God tell to go and marry a prostitute?

_____

23. What is the name of the Bible character who saw a roll flying in the sky?

_____

24. Two men in the Bible had the same name. One was a very poor man and the other was a friend of Jesus. What was their common name?

_____

25. When Peter was released from prison, he knocked at the door of the gate and a certain person came to answer his knock. Who was that individual?

_____

26. People will be thrown into the lake of fire because

_____.

27. When Paul was shipwrecked on the island of Melita, he stayed with the chief man on the island. Who was this man?

_____

28. What is the name of the man who slept in the land of Nod?

_____

29. "And they gave forth their lots; and the lot fell upon

_____; and he was numbered with the eleven apostles."

30. What was the name of the vagabond Jewish exorcist who tried to cast the evil spirit out of a man? "And the man in whom the evil spirit was leaped on them, and

overcame them, and prevailed against them, so that they fled out of that house naked and wounded."

31. "And Cush begat _____. He was a mighty hunter before the Lord."

32. What was the name of the queen that was replaced by Esther? _____

33. What Bible character was called "The Tishbite"?

34. Who in the Bible asked God to put his tears in a bottle?

35. What was the name of the archangel who debated with the devil?

36. What does the word Ichabod mean?

37. The apostle Peter was known by three names. What were they?

38. What was the name of the runaway slave who went back to his master?

39. Who said, "Am I a dog, that thou comest to me with staves"?

_____

40. What is the name of the partially blind man who was ninety-eight years old and was very fat who fell off his seat and broke his neck?

_____

41. What is the shortest verse in the Bible?

_____

42. What Bible character accidentally hanged himself in a tree?

_____

43. How many children did Jacob have?
    a. 9   b. 11   c. 13   d. 15   e. 17

44. How many days was Noah on the Ark before it started to rain?

_____

45. What type of bird fed the prophet Elijah?

_____

46. What is the longest chapter in the Bible?

_____

47. In what book of the Bible do you find the following words: "Can the Ethiopian change his skin, or the leopard his spots"?

_____

48. When a certain king put on a feast, God's handwriting appeared on the wall and startled everyone present. What is the name of this king?

_____

49. What is the name of the woman who slept at the feet of her future husband?

_____

50. What type of food did the brothers of Joseph eat after they threw him into the pit?

_____

51. A scarlet cord in a window saved someone and their family. Who was this person?

_____

52. In a contest for good-looking men, four men won because they were vegetarians and God blessed them. Who were these men?

_____

53. Elisha cursed forty-two children because they made fun of him and mocked him. What did they say?

_____

54. As a result of the curse of Elisha, what happened to the forty-two children?

_____

55. When God expelled Adam and Eve from the Garden of

    Eden, he placed Cherubim at the _____ of the Garden of Eden.

56. What Bible character drove his chariot furiously?

_____

57. What is the name of the left-handed Benjamite who killed King Eglon?

_____

58. King Eglon was killed with a dagger that was _____ inches long, and the dagger could not be pulled out

    because _____.

59. What two books in the Bible were written to Theophilus?

_____

60. What Bible character had his lips touched with a live coal?

_____

61. Who was the person who dreamed about a tree which reached to heaven?

_____

62. What woman in the Bible had five husbands?

_____

63. When the magi came to seek Baby Jesus, where did they find Him?

_____

64. Who caused bricklayers to go on strike?

_____

65. What Bible character changed dust into lice?

_____

66. Who was the man to first organize an orchestra in the Bible?

_____

67. Of all the books in the Bible, which one does not contain the name of God?

_____

68. A lost ax head was made to float by _____

_____.

69. What person in the Bible walked for forty days without eating?

_____

70. Why did Absalom kill his brother Amnon?

_____

71. Who paid for the nursing of Moses?

_____

72. Who committed suicide with his own sword?

_____

73. Who committed suicide by hanging himself?

_____

74. What king pouted in his bed because he could not buy
someone's vineyard? _____

75. King Solomon had another name. What was it?

_____

76. Who was the man to build the first city and what was its
name?

_____

77. What woman in the Bible made a pair of kid gloves for
her son? _____

78. A certain queen's blood was sprinkled on horses. Who
was this queen?

_____

79. Who was the first musician in the Bible? What instruments did he play?

_____

80. What Bible person cut his hair only once a year?

_____

81. Name the gentile king who made Esther his queen.

_____

82. Who said the following and to whom was he speaking? "Because thou hast mocked me: I would there were a sword in mine hand, for now would I kill thee."

_____

83. The mother-in-law of Ruth was Naomi. What was the name of her father-in-law?

_____

84. What is the name of the man who was seduced by his daughter-in-law and what was her name?

_____

85. How many times did Balaam hit his donkey before the donkey spoke to him?

_____

86. How many years were added to Hezekiah's life?

_____

87. Joash was told to shoot an arrow from the window. What was the arrow called?

_____

88. God gave Hezekiah a sign that he would live longer. What was that sign?

_____

89. Name the king who had the longest reign in the Bible.

_____

90. Which of the prophets was thrown into a dungeon?

_____

91. When a certain king tried to take the place of the priest at the altar, he was struck with leprosy. Who was this king?

_____

92. How was Naaman healed of his leprosy?

_____

93. While _____ was hanging in a tree, he was killed by three darts from Joab.

94. Nicodemus put how many pounds of myrrh and aloes on the body of Jesus?

_____

95. What was the name of the person who became king while he was a little child?

_____

96. Job's friends sat in silence with Job and mourned with him for how many days?

_____

97. Where was Judas Iscariot buried?

_____

98. Jesus told Nathanael that he had seen him before. Where did Jesus see Nathanael?

_____

99. In the book of Proverbs, God says he hates how many things?

_____

100. The Bible suggests that the average life span is how many years?

_____

101. How many barrels of water did Elijah ask the men to pour over the sacrifice on the altar?

_____

102. Because of offering "strange fire" on the altar of God, how many men died?

_____

103. David disobeyed God and numbered the people. As a
    result God gave David the choice of one of

    a. 2   b. 3   c. 4   d. 5

    different kinds of punishment.

104. What leader chose his followers by watching how they
    drank water?

    _____

105. How many stones were placed in the Jordan River after
    the children of Israel had crossed over on dry land?

    _____

106. As Joshua and the children of Israel marched around
    the walls of Jericho, the priests carried trumpets before
    the Ark of the Lord. How many priests carried trumpets?

    _____

107. When Elijah was on Mt. Carmel, how many times did
    he send his servant to look for a cloud?

    _____

108. The two spies that Rahab hid fled into the mountains
    and hid for how many days?

    _____

109. How many men from the tribe of Judah were sent out
    to capture Samson?

    _____

110. How old was Jehoash when he was crowned king?

_____

111. This person was brought water from the well at Bethlehem but poured it out on the ground because it was brought to him at great risk. Who was this person?

_____

112. What type of bird was sold for "two for a farthing"?

_____

113. Absalom was riding on a _____ when his hair caught in a tree.

114. What did Achan steal from Jericho?

_____

115. What Old Testament character wore a "coat of mail"?

_____

116. Name the twelve apostles.

_____

_____

_____

117. What was the name of the witch that Saul visited?

_____

118. The word "coffin" is used only once in the entire Bible
     Do you know who was buried in this coffin?

     _____

119. The Bible warns men to beware of a woman's eyes. In
     what book of the Bible do you find this warning?

     _____

120. While Joseph was in prison he interpreted dreams for
     two men. What were the occupations of these two
     men?

     _____

121. Whose birthday celebration was the first mentioned in
     the Bible?

     _____

122. In what book of the Bible does it talk about trading a
     boy for a harlot?

     _____

123. How many men in the Bible were named Judas?

     _____

124. Who received the first kiss that is mentioned in the
     Bible?

     _____

125. "The men of _____ were wicked and sinners
     before the Lord exceedingly."

126. In what book of the Bible do we find the first mention of a physician?

_____

127. When Jeremiah said that all their heads would be shaved and their beards clipped, who was he speaking about?

_____

128. Whose lips quivered and bones decayed when he heard the voice of the Lord?

_____

129. In what book of the Bible do you find the words, "Thine eyes like the fishpools in Heshbon"?

_____

130. Who was the first man the Bible says had a dream?

_____

131. In what book of the Bible do we find God's punishment of "consumption, and the burning ague"?

_____

132. How many chapters are in the book of Esther?

_____

133. How much money did the innkeeper receive from the Good Samaritan for taking care of the sick man?

_____

134. In what book of the Bible do we find the first mention of a "lunatic"?

_____

135. King Solomon had how many horsemen?

_____

136. In what book of the Bible do we have the first mention of magicians?

_____

137. Who does the Bible say eats, wipes her mouth, and says, "I've done nothing wrong"?

_____

138. What did David do with Goliath's weapons?

_____

139. In the end of the book of Job, how many camels did God give to Job?

_____

140. When Elijah built the altar on Mount Carmel, how many stones did he use?

_____

141. What were the names of Pharaoh's two store cities in the book of Exodus?

_____

142. In the book of Ruth, what was Naomi's other name?

_____

143. In what book of the Bible does God say there will be showers of blessing?

_____

144. In which book of the Bible do you read the words, "Be sure your sin will find you out"?

_____

145. Nabal owned how many goats?

_____

146. When Josiah heard God's law read, he did what?

_____

147. In what book of the Bible do we find mention of 20,000 baths of wine and 20,000 baths of oil?

_____

148. In Zechariah's vision of four chariots, what was the color of the horses pulling the fourth chariot?

_____

149. One book in the Bible has the same amount of chapters as there are books in the Bible. What is the name of the book?

_____

150. What was the name of Jonah's father?

_____

151. How many chapters are in the book of Nehemiah?

_____

152. What was the occupation of Shiphrah and Puah?

_____

153. What animal was never to be cooked in its mother's

milk? __ _____ _____

154. Rahab the harlot hid the two Jewish spies under what?

_____

155. What are the names of the two women who argued over who would get to sleep with their mutual husband?

_____

156. Miriam played what kind of musical instrument?

_____

157. What does the Bible say manna tasted like?

_____

158. What Bible character was called a wild donkey of a man?

_____

159. When King Nebuchadnezzar went crazy, his fingernails began to look like _____.

160. What is the last word in the Bible?

_____

161. What Bible character fell in love with his sister?

_____

162. The prophet Amos tended two things. What were they?

_____

163. The Ark of the Testimony or Covenant was covered with what color cloth when it was moved?

_____

164. Who was the first Bible character mentioned as living in a tent?

_____

165. What is the name of the Bible character who ran faster than a chariot?

_____

166. What three colors were used in sewing the tabernacle curtains?

_____

167. Who came out with bald heads and raw shoulders after a long siege against the city of Tyre?

_____

168. At what time of day did the sailors going to Rome on the ship with Paul first sense land after the storm?

_____

169. In the book of Acts, how many soldiers guarded Peter while he was in prison?

_____

170. Who was the first man in the Bible mentioned as being sick?

_____

171. Who was the fourth oldest man in the Bible?

_____

172. How many yoke of oxen did Job own before tragedy entered his life?

_____

173. In Elim, the Israelites found 70 palm trees and _____ springs (fountains).

174. Moses was told by the Lord to write what on the staff of each leader of the tribes of Israel?

_____

175. Hannah was taunted by _____ about not having a baby.

176. Certain Athenian philosophers thought Paul the apostle was a _____.

177. Zechariah had a vision of a basket (ephah). What was in the basket?

_____

178. When King Shishak stole the gold shields from the temple, who replaced them with bronze (brass) shields?

_____

179. In what book of the Bible do we find mention of the name Narcissus?

_____

180. In what book of the Bible do you find the words, "The joy of the Lord is my strength"?

_____

181. Who is the first person in the Bible mentioned as writing a letter?

_____

182. Who received the first letter written in the Bible?

_____

183. Who said, "If I perish, I perish"?

_____

184. Name the shortest book in the Old Testament.
   a. Jonah   b. Nehemiah   c. Obadiah
   d. Zephaniah   e. Malachi

185. The Recabites refused to drink _____.

186. The woman who poured perfume on Jesus' head carried the perfume in what kind of jar?

_____

187. Who does the Bible say was the most humble man?

_____

188. Who was Asenath's famous husband?

_____

189. Who bored a hole in the lid of a chest so that it could become a bank to hold money?

_____

190. After feeding the 4000 men, Jesus went where?

_____

191. what is the name of the prophet who said that Paul would be arrested in Jerusalem?

_____

192. When the temple in the Old Testament was moved, what kind of animal skins were put over the Ark of the Testimony or Covenant?

_____

193. What was the name of the dying king who was propped up in his chariot for a whole day?

_____

194. The Anakites (Anakims—KJV) and the Emites (Emims—KJV) had a common physical characteristic. What was it?

_____

195. King Solomon had his carriage upholstered in what color of material?

_____

196. In which book of the Bible do we find the first mention of the name Satan?

_____

197. The invalid had been lying by the pool of Bethesda for how many years?

_____

198. Mary washed Jesus' feet with what kind of perfume?

_____

199. What did Jacob name the place where he wrestled with a man?

_____

200. When Jacob wrestled with a man, what were the man's first words to Jacob?

_____

201. How many men did Esau bring with him when he came to meet Jacob?

    a. 100   b. 200   c. 300
    d. 400   e. 500

202. What special physical feature did Leah have?

_____

203. Elisha was plowing the ground with how many yoke of oxen when Elijah found him?

_____

204. In what book of the Bible does it talk about people who could not tell their right hand from their left hand?

_____

205. What is the name of the man who raped Dinah?

_____

206. When Job became ill, his skin turned to what color?

_____

207. David's delegation to King Hanun had to stay in what town until their beards had grown back?

_____

208. What woman's name is mentioned most often in the Bible?

_____

209. Gideon was the father of how many sons?

_____

210. What is the name of the king who had 900 iron chariots?

_____

211. King Solomon had how many steps to his throne?

_____

212. What was the name of Isaiah's father?

_____

213. David was betrothed to Saul's daughter for how many Philistine foreskins?

_____

214. After the Philistines cut off Saul's head, they put it in the temple of _____.

215. Deborah, the Old Testament judge, sat under what kind of tree?

_____

216. In the parable of the Good Samaritan, who was the second person to ignore the injured man?

_____

217. When King Ben-Hadad attacked Samaria, how many kings helped him?

_____

218. Jonathan, Ishvi, and Malki-Shua had a famous father. What was his name?

_____

219. What is the name of the Bible prophet who was lifted by his hair between heaven and earth to see a vision?

_____

220. What name did Amos call the sinful women of Israel?

_____

221. Nehemiah went to the keeper of the king's forest to get wood. What was the forest-keeper's name?

_____

222. When is the first time love is mentioned in the Bible?

_____

223. In which book of the Bible do we find the only mention of the name Lucifer?

   _____

224. What Bible character said, "By my God have I leaped over a wall"?

   _____

225. Who was the first left-handed man mentioned in the Bible?

   _____

226. Who called Israel a "backsliding heifer"?

   _____

227. Who said, "Man is born into trouble, as the sparks fly upward"?

   _____

228. The river Pishon flowed out of the Garden of Eden into the land _____, where there was gold.

229. In what book of the Bible do we find mention of the word stargazers?

   _____

230. The name "Ziz" was _____
   a. A city   b. A brook   c. A cliff
   d. A soldier   e. A priest   f. None of the
                                         above

231. Jazer was _____.

    a. A king   b. A land   c. A priest
    d. A river   e. A servant   f. None of the
                                         above

232. How old was Adam when he died?

233. Who was the father of Enoch?

234. How many days after the tops of the mountains appeared did Noah wait before he opened the window of the Ark?

235. Who was the famous son of Terah?

236. When Lot left Sodom, what city did he flee to?

237. What are the names of the two children who were born to Lot's two daughters?

238. How old was Sarah when she died?

    a. 103   b. 112   c. 127   d. 133

239. What were the names of the two wives of Esau who caused Isaac and Rebekah much grief?

240. Who was the second oldest man in the Bible?

241. How old was Enoch when God took him to heaven?

242. The Israelites hung their harps on what kind of trees?

243. After baptizing the eunuch, Philip was taken by the Spirit of the Lord to what city?

244. How long did Job live after the Lord made him prosperous again?

245. What was the name of Eli's grandson?

TRIVIA QUESTIONS
FOR THE EXPERT

1. What Bible personality was called a half-baked pancake?

   _____

2. What was the name of the king who put Jeremiah into a dungeon in which he sank in the mire?

   _____

3. Absalom caught his hair in what kind of a tree?

   _____

4. Four rivers flowed out of the Garden of Eden. What are the names of these four rivers?

   _____

   _____

5. Eldad and Medad are famous because of:

   a. Their victory in battle
   b. Their prophecy
   c. Their rebellion against Moses
   d. Not in the Bible

6. Muppim, Huppim, and Ard were:

   a. Amramite gods
   b. The words of a chant of the priest of Baal
   c. Three men who rebelled
   d. The sons of Benjamin
   e. Not in the Bible

7. What was the name of the man who had his head cut off and thrown over a wall to Joab?

_____

8. What tribe had 700 left-handed men who could sling stones at a hair breadth and not miss?

_____

9. What was the name of the secretary of Paul the apostle who wrote the book of Romans for Paul?

_____

10. At Belshazzar's feast a hand wrote on the wall, *"Mene, Mene, Tekel, U-pharsin."* What was the interpretation of the words?

_____

11. What were the weather forecasts Jesus told the Pharisees and Sadducees?

_____

12. Who was the person called Candace?

_____

13. When the seventh seal was opened in the book of Revelation, there was silence in heaven for:

   a. A minute   b. A half-hour   c. An hour
   d. A day   e. A month   f. A half-year
   g. A year

14. In His ministry, Jesus mentioned a region of ten cities. What was that region called?

_____

15. What was the name of Blind Bartimaeus's father?

_____

16. In what book of the Bible does God tell a certain man not to cover his mustache?

_____

17. When Aaron's rod blossomed, what type of nuts did it yield?

_____

18. On the priestly garments a certain fruit was used as a design. What kind of fruit was it?

_____

19. The Old Testament character Job lived in the land of
_____.

20. Who had faces like lions and could run as fast as the gazelles?

_____

21. What does the word Ebenezer mean?

_____

22. Who fell asleep during a sermon and died as a result?

_____

23. When the Ark of the Covenant was being brought back to Jerusalem, the oxen shook the cart and the Ark started to turn over. One man put his hand on the Ark to keep if from falling and died as a result of touching the Ark. Who was this man?

_____

24. What is the shortest verse in the Old Testament?

_____

25. Who were the people called the Zamzummims?

_____

26. The first archer mentioned in the Bible was _____.

27. There are four different colored horses mentioned in the book of Revelation. What were the four different colors?

_____

28. What Bible character called himself "a dead dog"?

_____

29. What evangelist had four daughters who prophesied?

_____

30. What is the longest word in the Bible?

_____

31. What king slept in a bed that was four cubits (six feet) wide and nine cubits (thirteen feet) long?

_____

32. In the book of Revelation a star called _____ fell when the third angel sounded his trumpet.

33. What little-boy king had to be hidden in a bedroom for six years to escape the wrath of his wicked grandmother?

_____

34. The giant Goliath lived in what city?

_____

35. How many proverbs is King Solomon credited in knowing?

_____

36. Who washed his steps with butter?

_____

37. Jeremiah had a secretary. What was his name?

_____

38. Who in the Bible is considered the father of all musicians?

_____

39. What is the name of the dressmaker who was raised from the dead?

_____

40. What Bible character's hair stood up on end when he

saw a ghost? _____

41. Naomi had two daughters-in-law. One daughter-in-law, Ruth, went with Naomi and the other daughter-in-law,

named _____, stayed in the country of Moab.

42. When Joshua destroyed Jericho he destroyed everyone in the city except for how many households?

_____

43. In what book of the Bible do you find a verse that contains every letter except the letter "J"?

_____

44. Most young men smile when they kiss a girl, but what Bible character wept when he kissed his sweetheart?

_____

45. What man in the Bible killed sixty-nine (threescore and nine) of his brothers?

_____

46. How much money did the brothers of Joseph make when they sold Joseph into slavery?

_____

47. What Bible-song composer is given credit for writing 1005 songs?

_____

48. Who were Jannes and Jambres?

   a. Two of the spies to the Promised Land
   b. Two priests in Israel
   c. Two men who started a rebellion against Joshua
   d. Two of Pharaoh's magicians
   e. Two of the children of Reuben

49. In order to bind a contract, what Bible person took off his shoe and gave it to his neighbor?

_____

50. What is the name of the five-year-old boy who was dropped by his nurse and became crippled for life?

_____

51. What woman in the Bible gave a man butter and then killed him by driving a nail through his head?

_____

52. Two lawyers are mentioned in the Bible. What are their names?

_____

53. What is the name of the king who became herbivorous and ate grass like the oxen?

_____

54. In what book of the Bible is bad breath mentioned?

_____

55. How long did Noah remain in the Ark?

_____

56. Who could use bows and arrows or sling stones with either the right or left hand?

_____

57. Who killed a lion in a pit on a snowy day?

_____

58. Who killed 300 men with his own spear?

_____

59. What Bible character ate a book and thought it was sweet like honey?

_____

60. Who was quoted for saying, "Is there any taste in the white of an egg?"

_____

61. During what event in the Bible did dove manure sell for food?

_____

62. How many different arks are mentioned in the Bible?

_____

63. What Bible character was mentioned as being the first craftsman with brass and iron?

_____

64. What is the shortest chapter in the Bible?

_____

65. What is the name of the individual who ate a little book and got indigestion?

_____

66. Adam called his helpmate woman and he named her Eve. What did God call Eve?

_____

67. What Bible character walked around naked and without

shoes for three years? _____

68. What is the name of the man who was killed by having a nail driven through his head?

_____

69. Who said, *"Eli, Eli, Lama sabachthani"* and what does it mean?

_____

_____

70. The Bible characters Samson, David, and Benaiah all have one thing in common. What is it?

_____

71. What was the name of the man who killed 800 men with a spear?

_____

72. Jesus had how many brothers and sisters?

_____

73. Who was the man that killed 600 men with an ox goad?

_____

74. What man in the Bible wished that he had been aborted?

_____

75. The ministering women gave up their brass mirrors to make a bathtub for men to wash in. Who were these men?

_____

76. What man in the Bible had hair like eagle feathers and nails like bird claws?

_____

77. How many people in the Bible have their name beginning with the letter "Z"?

_____

78. What was the name of the king who practiced divination by looking in a liver?

_____

79. How many men in the Bible are named Dodo?

_____

80. What was used to join the tabernacle curtains together?

_____

81. What was the name of the eight-year-old boy who served as king of Jerusalem for 100 days?

_____

82. What man tore his clothes and pulled out his hair because of interracial marriage?

_____

83. What man tore out other men's hair for interracial marriage?

_____

84. Who was the first bigamist to be mentioned in the Bible?

_____

85. What was the name of the judge in Israel who was a polygamist?

_____

86. What event caused a donkey's head to be sold for eighty pieces of silver?

_____

87. In what book of the Bible does it talk about camels wearing necklaces?

_____

88. Who fashioned five mice out of gold?

_____

89. In what portion of the Bible does it talk about the sole of a dove's foot?

_____

90. Who was the first drunkard to be talked about in the Bible?

_____

91. In what book in the Bible does it talk about men who neighed after their neighbors' wives?

_____

92. In the Old Testament 42,000 were killed for the incorrect pronunciation of one word. What was that word?

_____

93. What Bible character shot an arrow through a man's body and who was the man who died?

_____

94. What is the name of the man who fed seventy kings at his table?

_____

95. Who got so hungry that she ate her own son?

_____

96. What was queen Esther's other name?

_____

97. There is one place in the Bible where it talks about grease. In what book of the Bible do you find that comment?

_____

98. In what book of the Bible does it command brides to shave their heads and manicure their nails?

_____

99. According to Matthew, who were Joses, Simon, Judas, and James?

_____

100. Who killed a seven-and-a-half-foot tall Egyptian giant?

_____

101. Where is the swimmer's breaststroke mentioned in the Bible?

_____

102. Twenty-seven-thousand men were killed when a wall of a city fell on them. What was the name of the city where the wall was located?

_____

103. What was the name of the man who killed a giant having twelve fingers and twelve toes?

_____

104. What Bible character burned his son alive as a sacrifice?

_____

105. What person in the Bible set fire to 300 foxes' tails?

_____

106. What Bible character had neither a father nor mother, is mentioned eleven times in Scripture, was not born and did not die?

_____

107. The book of Proverbs lists four creatures that are small but exceedingly wise. What are these four creatures?

_____

108. Who warned his enemies by cutting up a yoke of oxen and saying to them that if they did not submit to him, the same thing would happen to them?

_____

109. After Jesus had risen from the dead, Peter was fishing and caught a large amount of fish in his net and brought them to Jesus. How many fish did Peter catch in his net?

_____

110. What Bible prophet prophesied that men would eat their own flesh?

_____

111. What person in the Bible said, "A living dog is better than a dead lion"?

_____

112. Which king set fire to his own palace and died in the flames?

_____

113. How many locks of hair did Delilah cut from Samson's hair?

_____

114. The prophet Ahijah the Shilonite found _____ outside of Jerusalem and tore his new garment into

_____ pieces.

115. What was the name of one of the two friends that met Jesus on the road to Emmaus after the resurrection?

_____

116. The word "ball" is mentioned only one time in the Bible. In what book of the Bible do you find this word?

_____

117. Jerusalem was also known by two other names. What were those names?

_____

118. How many pieces of silver did the Philistines promise Delilah if she could find out the secret of Samson's

strength? _____

119. Who saw the portraits of handsome young men and fell in love with what she saw?

_____

120. Where do you find the longest verse in the Bible?

_____

121. How did Michal, David's wife, help David to escape the king's messengers?

_____

122. What prophet talked about a girl being exchanged for a

drink (wine)? _____

123. What was the name of the Bible character who had seventy-eight wives and concubines who gave birth to eighty-eight children?

_____

124. There was a certain king who had his women perfumed for a year before they came to him. What was his name? _____

125. Nahor's two eldest sons were named:

    a. Huz and Buz   b. Huz and Muz   c. Buz and Muz
    d. Fuz and Suz   e. Huz and Fuz   f. Buz and Suz

126. Who were the men of whom God said, "Thou shalt make for them girdles, and bonnets"?

_____

127. Which book in the Bible talks about men who "belch out with their mouth"?

_____

128. In what book of the Bible does it talk about ice coming out of the womb?

_____

129. Who laughed when threatened with a spear?

_____

130. In what book of the Bible do we find mention of "wimples and the crisping pins"?

_____

131. What is the name of the Bible character who had 30 sons who rode on 30 donkeys and controlled 30 cities?

_____

132. In what book of the Bible do we have the first mention of a barber's razor?

133. The angel of the Lord killed how many of Sennacherib's soldiers?

134. How many times is the Old Testament quoted in the book of Revelation?

135. In what verse of the Bible do we find the word "cankerworm" mentioned twice?

136. In what book of the Bible do we find the only two occurrences of the word rainbow?

137. In what book of the Bible do we read the words, "Twisting the nose produces blood" (NIV)?

138. What is the name of the Bible character who said, "I have escaped with only the skin of my teeth" (NIV)?

139. According to King Solomon, good news gives health to what part of our body?

_____

140. How long did Ezekiel lie on his right side for the sins of Judah?

_____

141. What book of the Bible talks about "five gold tumors and five gold rats" (NIV)?

_____

142. The bronze snake that Moses made was broken into pieces by what king?

_____

143. What Bible character was smothered to death by a wet cloth?

_____

144. Which chapter in the book of Psalms could be a statement against abortion?

_____

145. What book of the Bible talks about a man "that hath a flat nose"?

_____

146. What Bible character was known for his threats to gouge out the right eye of the people who lived in Jabesh Gilead?

_____

147. How close to the city of Jericho was the brook of Ziba?

_____

148. Who was the high priest when Nehemiah rebuilt the walls of Jerusalem?

_____

149. How many men did Solomon use to cut stone for the temple?

_____

150. The Bible says that what bird is cruel to her young?

_____

151. God spoke to Jeremiah and said something that is a good argument against abortion. What was that statement?

_____

152. What was the name of Ezekiel's father?

_____

153. What Bible character thought laughter was a foolish thing?

_____

154. In what book of the Bible do you find the first mention of using battering rams against gates of a city?

_____

155. God showed a basket to the prophet Amos. What was in that basket?

_____

156. The word eternity is used _____ times in the Bible.

157. Ahab's 70 sons had their heads cut off and sent in baskets to what man?

_____

158. Which Bible character had the first king-sized bed?

_____

159. In which two books of the Bible do we read about cannibalism?

_____

160. Which family in the Bible did not have to pay taxes?

_____

161. The Bible says that storks build their nests in what kind of trees?

_____

162. How did God destroy the kings who attacked Gibeon?

_____

163. In what book of the Bible does it talk about nose jewelry?

_____

164. What Bible character had this thumbs and big toes cut off by the tribes of Judah and Simeon?

_____

165. What Bible character hid his belt (girdle—KJV) in the crevice of the rocks?

_____

166. What is the name of the young virgin who kept King David warm during his old age?

_____

167. King Saul sat under what kind of tree while Jonathan went to attack the Philistines?

_____

168. What was the name of Abraham's servant?

_____

169. How many chapters are there in the entire Bible?

_____

170. Who was the father of Ziddim, Zer, Hammath, Rakkath, and Kinnereth?

_____

171. How many chapters are there in the Old Testament?

_____

172. What Bible character was beheaded, cremated, and then buried?

_____

173. In what book of the Bible do we find mention of "mufflers"?

_____

174. Gideon received golden earrings as payment for conquering the Midianites. How much did the earrings weigh?

_____

175. What is the most used word in the Bible?

_____

176. The valley of Siddim was famous for what?

_____

177. Where was Ishbosheth's head buried?

_____

178. When the tabernacle was built, who was the chief craftsman?

_____

179. What emotion will cause your bones to rot?

_____

180. What group of people were told to burn their hair after it was cut off?

_____

181. Who was told to say, "My little finger is thicker than my father's waist" (NIV)?

_____

182. In what book of the Bible do you find the "hill of the foreskins"?

_____

183. Hezekiah had a poultice put on his boil. What was the poultice made of?

_____

184. What was the name of Goliath's brother?

_____

185. What three things did the Pharisees and scribes tithe?

_____

186. What are the names of the two women who had their ages recorded in the Bible?

_____

187. What was the name of the eunuch who was in charge of King Xerxes' (King Ahasuerus—KJV) concubines?

_____

188. What Bible character is mentioned as having an incurable bowel disease?

_____

189. What Bible character said that soldiers should be content with their pay?

_____

190. The horses of the Babylonians (Chaldeans—KJV) were likened to what kind of animals?

a. Lions   b. Leopards   c. Deer
d. Sheep   e. Eagles

191. What did Moses throw into the air to signal the start of the plague of boils on Egypt?

_____

192. In what book of the Bible do we find mention of "round tires like the moon"?

_____

193. In Zechariah's vision, the man on the red horse was riding among what kind of trees?

_____

194. What is the name of the man who tried to humiliate David's army by cutting off half of each soldier's beard and their garments in the middle at the buttocks?

    _____

195. What is the name of the man who wrote Proverbs 30?

    _____

196. In the book of Revelation, Antipas was martyred in

    _____ for his faith.

197. How many Bible characters are mentioned as living over 900 years?

    a. 3   b. 5   c. 7   d. 9   e. 11

198. Solomon made the steps of the temple and the palace out of what kind of wood?

    _____

199. What were the first words Elisha spoke when he saw Elijah going to heaven?

    _____

200. How many suicides are mentioned in the Bible?

    _____

201. The wicked King Abimelech was critically injured by a

    woman dropping a _____ on his head.

202. How many days was Ezekiel told to lie on his side while eating only bread and water?

_____

203. King Asa had what kind of disease?

_____

204. God punished David for taking a census of the people. How many people died in God's punishment?

_____

205. The Israelites were told not to destroy what when they besieged cities in the Old Testament?

_____

206. How many shekels of silver did Achan steal?

_____

207. The name Judas Iscariot appears how many times in the Bible?

_____

208. When Rachel stole some household gods from her father, she hid them in a camel's saddle and sat on the saddle. When her father came looking for the images, what excuse did Rachel use for not getting off the camel's saddle?

_____

209. Obadiah hid _____ prophets in caves to protect them from Jezebel.

210. When the tower of Siloam fell, how many people were killed? _____

211. What Bible character talks about beautiful feet?

_____

212. In what book of the Bible does it say, "Our skin was black like an oven because of the terrible famine"?

_____

213. In what book of the Bible do we find the famous verse, "At Parbar westward, four at the causeway, and two at Parbar"?

_____

214. What Bible character cooked his bread on cow dung?

_____

215. Name the only book in the Bible that is addressed specifically to a woman.

_____

216. How many people were shipwrecked with the apostle Paul in the book of Acts?

_____

217. Who was the famous father of Maher-Shalel-Hash-Baz? _____

218. What is the name of the king of Judah who made war machines that could shoot arrows and hurl huge stones?

_____

219. What was the name of Haman's wife?

_____

220. How many times does the name Satan appear in the Bible?

_____

221. The manna in the wilderness was likened to what kind of seed?

_____

222. What will bring "health to thy navel and marrow to thy bones"?

_____

223. Which town in the Bible had silver heaped up like dust and fine gold like the dirt of the streets?

_____

224. In what book of the Bible do we have mention of "sea

monsters"? _____

225. How many times is the word Lord mentioned in the Bible?

a. 5,017   b. 6,370   c. 7,736   d. 8,212   e. 9,108

226. In what two books of the Bible does it talk about men drinking their own urine and eating their own refuse?

_____

227. Which book of the Bible mentions men "fearing lest they should fall into the quicksands"?

_____

228. To whom did Ebed-melech, the Ethiopian say, "Put now these... rotten rags under thine armholes"?

_____

229. What man in the Bible did not shave or wash his clothes for many days? _____

230. Who grabbed Amasa by the beard with his right hand and pretended that he was going to kiss him, but instead stabbed him with a dagger?

_____

231. How many times is Beer mentioned in the Bible?

_____

232. In what book of the Bible do we have the only mention of a ferry boat?

_____

233. What two tribes built an altar between them and called it Ed?

_____

234. Where in the Bible does it talk about a gathering of the sheriffs?

_____

235. In which book of the Bible does it talk about melting slugs or snails? _____

236. How many times is the word "the" used in the Bible?
a. Over 9,000   b. Over 11,000   c. Over 14,000

237. In what book of the Bible do we find mention of stars singing?

_____

238. How many times is the word suburbs mentioned in the Bible?

_____

239. How many times are unicorns mentioned in the Bible?

_____

240. Who was the brother of Zered?

_____

241. If Cain was avenged sevenfold, how many times would Lamech be avenged?

_____

242. To how many people did God say, "Be fruitful, and multiply, and replenish the earth"?

_____

243. What time of day did God rain down fire and brimstone on Sodom and Gomorrah?

_____

244. What did Abraham call the name of the place where he was about to sacrifice Isaac?

_____

245. How old was Esau when he married his two wives Judith and Basemath?

_____

246. Isaiah prophesied that _____ women would take hold of one man.

247. Zechariah saw a vision of a scroll that was _____ feet long.

248. Who was the first man to say, "I have sinned" in the Bible?

_____

249. The Bible character Zaphenath-Paneah was known by another famous name. What was that name?

_____

250. In Zechariah's vision, the flying scroll was how wide?

_____

Puns, Riddles, and Humorous Trivia Questions

1. What was the name of Isaiah's horse?

   _____

2. Who was the first man in the Bible to know the meaning of rib roast?

   _____

3. Where does it talk about Honda cars in the Bible?

   _____

4. Who is the smallest man in the Bible?

   _____

5. Where in the Bible does it say that we should not play marbles?

   _____

6. How were Adam and Eve prevented from gambling?

   _____

7. Where does it say in the Bible that we should not fly in airplanes?

_____

8. What did Noah say while he was loading all the animals on the Ark?

_____

9. When did Moses sleep with five people in one bed?

_____

10. Where in the Bible does it talk about smoking?

_____

11. What was the first theatrical event in the Bible?

_____

12. Where in the Bible does it say that fathers should let their sons use the automobile?

_____

13. Why are there so few men with whiskers in heaven?

_____

14. Who was the best financier in the Bible?

_____

15. What simple affliction brought about the death of Samson?

_____

16. What did Adam and Eve do when they were expelled from the Garden of Eden?

_____

17. What are two of the smallest insects mentioned in the Bible?

_____

18. In what place did the cock crow when all the world could hear him?

_____

19. What were the Phoenicians famous for?

_____

20. Where is deviled ham mentioned in the Bible?

_____

21. Who introduced the first walking stick?

_____

22. Where is medicine first mentioned in the Bible?

_____

23. Where in the Bible does it suggest that men should wash dishes?

_____

24. Where did Noah strike the first nail in the Ark?

_____

25. Why was Moses the most wicked man in the Bible?

_____

26. What man in the Bible spoke when he was a very small

baby? _____

27. At what time of day was Adam born?

_____

28. What man in the Bible had no parents?

_____

29. Where is tennis mentioned in the Bible?

_____

30. Was there any money on Noah's Ark?

_____

31. Paul the apostle was a great preacher and teacher and earned his living as a tentmaker. What other occupation did Paul have?

_____

32. Why was Adam's first day the longest?

_____

33. Why was the woman in the Bible turned into a pillar of salt?

_____

34. What is the story in the Bible that talks about a very lazy man?

_____

35. Why didn't the last dove return to the Ark?

_____

36. Who was the most successful physician in the Bible?

_____

37. How do we know they used arithmetic in early Bible times?

_____

38. How long a period of time did Cain hate his brother?

_____

39. Who was the first electrician in the Bible?

_____

40. Who sounded the first bell in the Bible?

_____

41. How did Jonah feel when the great fish swallowed him?

_____

42. Why are a pair of roller skates like the forbidden fruit in the Garden of Eden?

_____

43. What does the story of Jonah and the great fish teach us?

_____

44. Do you know how you can tell that David was older than Goliath?

_____

45. What is the difference between Noah's Ark and an archbishop?

_____

46. When did Ruth treat Boaz badly?

_____

47. Where was Solomon's temple located?

_____

48. Who is the fastest runner in the world?

_____

49. If Moses were alive today, why would he be considered a remarkable man?

_____

50. How do we know that Noah had a pig in the Ark?

_____

51. Why did Moses cross the Red Sea?

_____

52. Who was the most popular actor in the Bible?

_____

53. Who was the most ambitious man in the Bible?

_____

54. Who were the twin boys in the Bible?

_____

55. Where is baseball mentioned in the Bible?

_____

56. Who was the first person in the Bible to eat herself out of house and home?

_____

57. Why was Job always cold in bed?

_____

58. How were the Egyptians paid for goods taken by the Israelites when they fled from Egypt?

_____

59. Why didn't they play cards on Noah's Ark?

_____

60. In the story of the Good Samaritan, why did the Levite pass by on the other side?

_____

61. Who was the straightest man in the Bible?

_____

62. Which came first—the chicken or the egg?

_____

63. When is high finance first mentioned in the Bible?

_____

64. What is the only wage that does not have any deductions?

_____

65. At what season of the year did Eve eat the fruit?

_____

66. If Methuselah was the oldest man in the Bible (969 years of age), why did he die before his father?

_____

67. What has God never seen, Abraham Lincoln seldom saw, and we see every day?

_____

68. On the Ark, Noah probably got milk from the cows. What did he get from the ducks?

_____

69. One of the first things Cain did after he left the Garden of Eden was to take a nap. How do we know this?

_____

70. Where do you think the Israelites may have deposited their money?

_____

71. Why do you think that the kangaroo was the most miserable animal on the Ark?

_____

72. What prophet in the Bible was a space traveler?

_____

73. What do you have that Cain, Abel, and Seth never had?

_____

74. What city in the Bible was named after something that you find on every modern-day car?

_____

75. When the Ark landed on Mount Ararat, was Noah the first one out?

_____

76. What was the difference between the 10,000 soldiers of Israel and the 300 soldiers Gideon chose for battle?

_____

77. Where is the first math problem mentioned in the Bible?

_____

78. Where is the second math problem mentioned in the Bible?

_____

79. Why did Noah have to punish and discipline the chickens on the Ark?

_____

80. What was the most expensive meal served in the Bible and who ate it?

_____

81. Certain days in the Bible passed by more quickly than most of the days. Which days were these?

_____

82. Matthew and Mark have something that is not found in Luke and John. What is it?

_____

83. Which one of Noah's sons was considered to be a clown?

_____

84. What is the first game mentioned in the Bible?

_____

85. What made Abraham so smart?

_____

86. What is most of the time black, sometimes brown or white, but should be red?

_____

87. Why did everyone on the Ark think that the horses were pessimistic?

_____

88. Who was the first person in the Bible to have surgery performed on him?

_____

89. When was the Red Sea very angry?

_____

90. What vegetable did Noah not want on the Ark?

_____

91. Why do you think Jonah could not trust the ocean?

_____

92. How do we know that God has a sense of humor?

_____

93. What time was it when the hippopotamus sat on Noah's rocking chair?

_____

94. What does God both give away and keep at the same time?

_____

95. During the six days of creation, which weighed more— the day or the night?

_____

96. What did the skunks on the Ark have that no other animals had?

_____

97. What type of tea does the Bible suggest that we not drink?

_____

98. In what book of the Bible do we find something that is in modern-day courtrooms?

_____

99. Which animal on the Ark was the rudest?

_____

100. What kind of soap did God use to keep the oceans clean?

_____

101. How do we know that the disciples were very cruel to the corn?

_____

102. Why did the rooster refuse to fight on the Ark?

_____

103. Why didn't Cain please the Lord with his offering?

_____

104. One of the names of the books of the Bible contains an insect in it. Which one is it?

_____

105. How many animals could Noah put into the empty Ark?

_____

106. Which man in the Bible might have only been 12 inches?

_____

107. Which book in the Bible is the counting book?

_____

108. What kind of lights did Noah have on the Ark?

_____

109. Gideon had 70 sons. How many of them were big men when they were born?

_____

110. Which candle burns longer—the candle hidden under a bushel or the candle set on a hill?

_____

111. Which animal on Noah's Ark had the highest level of intelligence?

_____

112. What indication is there that there may have been newspaper reporters in the New Testament?

_____

113. The name of one book of the Bible contains an ugly old woman. Which book is it?

_____

114. Which animal on the Ark did Noah not trust?

_____

115. Which Bible character was as strong as steel?

_____

116. What man in the Bible is named after a chicken?

_____

117. Where does the Bible suggest that it is okay to be overweight?

_____

118. What Bible character has a name that rang a bell?

_____

119. Which bird on Noah's Ark was a thief?

_____

120. Where does the Bible suggest that newspapers, magazines, radio, and television are powerful?

_____

121. What is the name of the individual who was perfect in the Bible?

_____

122. What was Eve's formal name?

_____

123. On Noah's Ark, why did the dog have so many friends?

_____

124. Who killed a fourth of all the people in the world?

_____

125. Where does it suggest that there may have been buses in the Bible?

_____

126. When Eve left the garden without Adam, what did Adam say?

_____

127. When a camel with no hump was born on the Ark, what did Noah name it?

_____

128. How long did Samson love Delilah?

_____

129. Where are freeways first mentioned in the Bible?

_____

130. What is the name of the sleepiest land in the Bible?

_____

131. What did Noah call the cat that fell into the pickle barrel on the Ark?

_____

132. What age were the goats when Adam named them in the Garden of Eden?

_____

133. David played a dishonest musical instrument. What was it called?

_____

134. Which of the Old Testament prophets were blind?

_____

135. How did Noah keep the milk from turning sour on the Ark?

_____

136. How many books in the Old Testament are named after Esther?

_____

137. What would have happened if all the women would have left the nation of Israel?

_____

138. Why did the giant fish finally let Jonah go?

_____

139. Why was Moses buried in a valley in the land of Moab near Bethpeor?

_____

140. The name of a book of the Bible contains a fruit. Which book is it?

_____

141. What is in the wall of Jerusalem that the Israelites did not put there?

_____

142. Why was the "W" the nastiest letter in the Bible?

_____

143. How did Joseph learn to tell the naked truth?

_____

144. What food did Samson eat to become strong?

_____

145. Why did the tower of Babel stand in the land of Shinar?

_____

146. Why did Moses have to be hidden quickly when he was a baby?

_____

147. Where in the Bible do we find the authority for women to kiss men?

_____

148. What two things could Samson the Nazarite never eat for breakfast?

_____

149. If Elijah was invited to dinner and was served only a beet, what would he say?

_____

150. If a man crosses the Sea of Galilee twice without a bath, what would he be?

_____

151. If someone wanted to be converted by John the Baptist, what was the first requirement?

_____

152. What day of the week was the best for cooking manna in the wilderness?

_____

153. If a soft answer turneth away wrath, what does a hard answer do?

_____

154. In what book of the Bible does it talk about people wearing tires on their heads?

_____

155. What is the golden rule of the animal world?

_____

156. How did Adam and Eve feel when they left the garden?

_____

157. Samson was a very strong man but there was one thing he could not hold for very long. What was that?

_____

158. If Moses would have dropped his rod in the Red Sea, what would it have become?

_____

159. What fur did Adam and Eve wear?

_____

160. Why must Elijah's parents have been good business people?

_____

161. Jesus and the giant fish that swallowed Jonah have something in common. What is it?

_____

162. What did Joseph in the Old Testament have in common
     with Zaccheus in the New Testament?

     _____

163. In what way does an attorney resemble a rabbi?

     _____

164. What does a Christian man love more than life;
     Hate more than death or mortal strife;
     That which contented men desire;
     The poor have, the rich require;
     The miser spends, the spendthrift saves;
     And all men carry to their graves?

     _____

165. What is that which Adam never saw or possessed, yet
     left two for each of his children?

     _____

166. What is greater than God, not as wicked as Satan, if
     people are alive and eat it they will die, and dead
     people eat it?

     _____

MELODY IN F
(THE PRODIGAL SON)

Feeling footloose and frisky, a
    featherbrained fellow
Forced his fond father to fork over the
    farthings.
And flew far to foreign fields
And frittered his fortune feasting
    fabulously with faithless friends.

Fleeced by his fellows in folly, and facing
    famine,
He found himself a feed-flinger in a filthy
    farmyard.
Fairly famishing, he fain would have filled
    his frame
With foraged food from fodder fragments.

"Fooey, my father's flunkies fare far
    finer,"
The frazzled fugitive forlornly fumbled,
    frankly facing facts.
Frustrated by failure, and filled with
    foreboding,
He fled forthwith to his family.
Falling at his father's feet, he forlornly
    fumbled,

"Father, I've flunked,
And fruitlessly forfeited family fellowship
    favor."

The farsighted father, forestalling further
    flinching,
Frantically flagged the flunkies to
Fetch a fatling from the flock and fix a
    feast.
The fugitives' faultfinding brother frowned
On fickle forgiveness of former folderol.

But the faithful father figured,
"Filial fidelity is fine, but the fugitive is
    found!
What forbids fervent festivity?
Let flags be unfurled! Let fanfares flare!"
Father's forgiveness formed the foundation
For the former fugitives' future fortitude!

THE BOOK OF PARABLES

Recently I interviewed some _____ (teachers, students or whoever) from _____ (name of church, school, or organization you are speaking to) and asked (them) some Bible questions. I could tell that they had really learned a great deal, so I asked them what their favorite book of the Bible was. They said, "The New Testament." I replied, "What part of the New Testament?" They said, "Oh, by far, we love the Book of Parables best." I said, "Would you kindly relate one of those parables to me."

They said, "Once upon a time, a man went from Jerusalem to Jericho and fell among thieves. And the thieves threw him into the weeds. And the weeds grew up and choked that man. He then went on and met the Queen of Sheba and she gave that man a thousand talents of gold and silver and a hundred changes of raiment. He then got in his chariot and drove furiously to the Red Sea. When he got there, the waters parted and he drove to the other side.

"On the other side he drove under a big olive tree and got his hair caught on a limb and was left hanging there. He hung there many days and many nights and the ravens brought him food to eat and water to drink. One night while he was hanging there asleep his wife Delilah came along and cut off his hair. And he dropped and fell on stony ground. And the children of a nearby city came out and said, 'Go up thou bald head, go up thou bald head.' And the man cursed the children and two she-bears came out of the woods and tore up the children.

"Then it began to rain and it rained for forty days and forty nights. And he went and hid himself in a cave. Later he went out and met a man and said, 'Come and take supper with me.' But the man replied, 'I cannot come for I have married a wife.' So he went out into the highways and byways and compelled them to come in, but they would not heed his call.

"He then went on to Jericho and blew his trumpet seven times and the city walls came tumbling down. As he walked by one of the damaged buildings in the city he saw Queen Jezebel sitting high up in a window and when she saw him she laughed and made fun of him. The man grew furious and said, 'Toss her down.' And they did. Then he said, 'Toss her down again.' And they did. They threw her down seventy times seven. And the fragments they gathered up were twelve baskets full. The question now is... 'Whose wife will she be on the day of resurrection?'"

THE CHRIST OF THE BIBLE

More than 1900 years ago there was a Man born contrary to the laws of life. This Man lived in poverty and was reared in obscurity. He did not travel extensively. Only once did He cross the boundary of the country in which He lived and that was during His exile in childhood.

He possessed neither name, wealth, nor influence. His relatives were inconspicuous, uninfluential, and had neither training nor education.

In infancy He startled a king; in childhood He puzzled the doctors; in manhood He ruled the course of nature, walked upon billows as if pavements, and hushed the sea to sleep.

He healed the multitudes without medicine and made no charge for His service.

He never wrote a book, and yet all the libraries of the country could not hold the books that have been written about Him.

He never wrote a song, and yet He has furnished the theme for more songs than all the songwriters combined.

He never founded a college, but all the schools put together cannot boast of having as many students.

He never practiced medicine, and yet He has healed more broken hearts than all the doctors far and near.

He never marshalled an army, nor drafted a soldier, nor fired a gun, and yet no leader ever had more volunteers who have, under His orders, made more rebels stack arms and surrender without a shot being fired.

He is the Star of astronomy, the Rock of geology, the Lion and Lamb of the zoological kingdom.

He is the Revealer of the snares that lurk in the darkness; and Rebuker of every evil thing that prowls by night; the Quickener of all that is wholesome; the Adorner of all that is beautiful; the Reconciler of all that is contradictory; the Harmonizer of all discords; the Healer of all diseases; and the Savior of all mankind.

He fills the pages of theology and hymnology. Every prayer that goes up to God goes up in His name and is asked to be granted for His sake.

Every seventh day the wheels of commerce cease their turning and multitudes wend their way to worshiping assemblies to pay homage and respect to Him.

The names of the past proud statesmen of Greece and Rome have come and gone. The names of the past scientists, philosophers, and theologians have come and gone; but the name of this Man abounds more and more. Though time has spread 1900 years between the people of this generation and the scene of His crucifixion, yet He still lives. Herod could not kill Him. Satan could not seduce Him. Death could not hold Him.

He stands forth upon the highest pinnacle of heavenly glory, proclaimed of God, acknowledged by angels, adored by saints, and feared by devils, as the living, personal Christ.

This Man, as you know, is Jesus Christ, our Lord and Savior!

A study of the Bible reveals Christ as its central subject and great theme. What the hub is to the wheel, Christ is to the Bible. It revolves around Him. All its types point to Him, all its truths converge in Him, all its glories reflect Him, all its promises radiate from Him, all its beauties are embodied by Him, all its demands are exemplified by Him, and all its predictions are accepted by Him.

Abel's lamb was a type of Christ. Abraham offering Isaac on Mount Moriah was a type of God giving Christ, His only Son, on Mount Calvary. The passover lamb in Egypt was a type of Christ. The brazen serpent in the wilderness was a type of Christ—He told Nicodemus so Himself. The scapegoat typified Him bearing our sins. The scarlet thread that the harlot Rahab hung in the window of her home in Jericho typified Him. Joseph, pictured to us by the Bible without a flaw, was a type of Christ "who did not sin, neither was guile found in his mouth."

In the Old Testament He is spoken of as "the angel of the Lord," and as such He appeared unto men.

He was with Adam and Eve in the Garden of Eden. He was with Abel in his death. He walked with Enoch. He rode with Noah in the Ark. He ate with Abraham in his desert tent. He pled with Lot to leave wicked Sodom.

He watched Isaac reopen the wells that his father Abraham had dug. He wrestled with Jacob at Peniel. He strengthened Joseph in his time of temptation, protected him in prison, and exalted him to first place in the kingdom. He watched over Moses in the ark of bulrushes, talked to him from the burning bush, went down into Egypt with him, opened the Red Sea for him, fed him on bread from heaven, protected him with a pillar of fire by night, and after 120 years of such blessed companionship that they left no marks of passing time upon Moses, led him up from the plains of Moab unto the mountain of Nebo, to the top of Pisgah, let him take one long, loving look at the Promised Land, and then kissed him to sleep, folded Moses' hands over his breast, and buried his body in an unmarked grave, to sleep in Jesus till the morning of the great resurrection day.

He was the Captain of the Lord's host to Joshua, led him over the swollen stream of Jordan in flood tide, around Jericho, in conquest of Ai, helped him conquer Canaan, divide the land, and say good-bye to the children of Israel. He was with Gideon and his famous 300. He was with

Samuel when he rebuked Saul. He was with David when he wrote the twenty-third psalm. He was with Solomon when he built the first temple. He was with good king Hezekiah when Sennacherib invaded the land. He was with Josiah in his great reformation that brought the people back to the law. He was with Ezekiel and Daniel in Babylon. He was with Jeremiah in Egypt. He was with Ezra when he returned from Babylon, and with Nehemiah when he rebuilt the wall. In fact, He was with all those "who through faith subdued kingdoms, wrought righteousness, obtained promises, stopped the mouths of lions, quenched the violence of fire, escaped the edge of the sword, out of weakness were made strong, waxed valiant in fight, turned to flight the armies of the aliens."

Abraham saw His day and rejoiced. Jacob called Him the "Lawgiver of Judah." Moses called Him the "Prophet that was to come." Job called Him "My Living Redeemer." Daniel called Him the "Ancient of Days." Jeremiah called Him "The Lord our Righteousness." Isaiah called Him "Wonderful Counselor, the Mighty God, the Everlasting Father, the Prince of Peace."

All of this in the Old Testament? Yes, and much more besides. "To Him give all the prophets witness." Micah tells of the place of His birth. Jonah tells of His death, burial, and resurrection. Amos tells of His second coming to build again the tabernacles of David. Joel describes the day of His wrath. Zechariah tells of His coming reign as King over all the earth. Ezekiel gives us a picture of His millennial temple.

In fact, my friends, it matters little where we wander down the aisles, avenues, byways, or highways of the Old Testament. Jesus walks beside us as He walked beside the two disciples on that dusty road to Emmaus on that glorious resurrection day long, long ago.

Its types tell of Him, its sacrifices show Him, its symbols signify Him, its histories are His-stories, its songs are His sentiments, its prophecies are His pictures, its promises are

His pledges; and our hearts burn within us as we walk beside Him across its living pages!

When we open the New Testament, the Word which was in the beginning with God becomes flesh and dwells among us, and we behold His glory, the glory as of the only begotten of the Father, full of grace and truth.

There are four personal histories of His earthly life written in the New Testament. One is by Matthew, the redeemed publican, and signifies His lineage; one is by Mark, the unknown servant, which magnifies His service; one is by Luke, "the beloved physician," and tells of His humanity; and one is by John, "whom Jesus loved," and it tells of His deity. He is Christ the King in Matthew, the Servant in Mark, the Man in Luke, and the Incarnate Word in John.

Concerning His royal lineage we learn that He was born in Bethlehem, the Seed of Abraham, the Son of David, the Son of Mary, the Son of God; and was acknowledged as "King of the Jews," "Christ the Lord," "God's Son," "The Savior of Men," by angels, demons, shepherds, and wise men; and that He received tribute of gold, frankincense, and myrrh.

Concerning His service we learn that He labored as a carpenter, opened eyes of the blind, unstopped deaf ears, loosed dumb tongues, cleansed lepers, healed the sick, restored withered hands, fed the hungry, sympathized with the sad, washed the disciples' feet, wept with Mary and Martha, preached the Gospel to the poor, went about doing good, and gave His life as a ransom for many.

Concerning His humanity we learn that He was born of a woman, as a little babe was wrapped in swaddling clothes, grew up and developed as a child in wisdom, stature, and in favor with God and men. He worked with His hands, He grew weary, He hungered, He thirsted, He slept, He felt the surge of anger; knew what it was to be sad, shed tears, sweat drops of blood; was betrayed, went though the mockery of a criminal trial, was scourged, had His hands and feet pierced; wore a crown of thorns, was spit upon, was crucified, was wrapped in a winding sheet, and was buried in a borrowed tomb behind a sealed stone, and was guarded by Roman soldiers in His death.

Concerning His deity we read that He was born of a virgin, lived a sinless life, spoke matchless words, stilled storms, calmed waves, rebuked winds, multiplied loaves, turned water to wine, raised the dead, foretold the future, gave hearing to the deaf, sight to the blind, speech to the dumb, cast out demons, healed diseases, forgave sins, claimed equality with God, arose from the dead, possessed all authority both in heaven and in earth.

He was both God and Man; two individuals united in one personality. "As a man, He thirsted; as God, He gave living water. As a man, He went to a wedding; as God, He turned the water to wine. As man, He slept in a boat; as God, He stilled the storm. As man, He was tempted; as God, He sinned not. As man, He wept; as God, He raised Lazarus from the dead. As man, He prayed; as God, He makes intercession for all men."

This is what Paul means when he writes, "Without controversy great is the mystery of godliness; God was manifest in the flesh, justified in the Spirit, seen of angels, preached unto the Gentiles, believed on in the world, received up into glory." He was made unto us wisdom, righteousness, sanctification, and redemption. He is the Light of this world. He is the Bread of Life. He is the True Vine. He is the Good Shepherd. He is the Way. He is the Life. He is the Door to Heaven.

He is the Faithful Witness, the First Begotten of the dead, the Prince of the kings of the earth, the King of Kings, and the Lord of lords, Alpha and Omega, the first and the last, the beginning and the ending, the Lord who is, who was, and who is to come, the Almighty. "I am He that liveth, and was dead; and behold, I am alive forevermore, and I have the keys of hell and of death."

He is the theme of the Bible from beginning to end: He is my Savior, let Him be your Savior, too!

In Genesis He is the Seed of the Woman

In Exodus He is the Passover Lamb

In Leviticus He is our High Priest

In Numbers He is the Pillar of Cloud by day and the Pillar of Fire by night

In Deuteronomy He is the Prophet like unto Moses

In Joshua He is the Captain of our Salvation

In Judges He is our Judge and Lawgiver

In Ruth He is our Kinsman Redeemer

In 1 and 2 Samuel He is our Trusted Prophet

In Kings and Chronicles He is our Reigning King

In Ezra He is the Rebuilder of the broken-down walls of human life

In Esther He is our Mordecai

And in Job He is our Ever-Living Redeemer, "For I know my redeemer liveth."

In Psalms He is our Shepherd

In Proverbs and Ecclesiastes He is our Wisdom

In the Song of Solomon He is our Lover and Bridegroom

In Isaiah He is the Prince of Peace

In Jeremiah He is the Righteous Branch

In Lamentations He is our Weeping Prophet

In Ezekiel He is the wonderful Four-Faced Man

And in Daniel the Fourth Man in "Life's Fiery Furnaces."

In Hosea He is the Faithful Husband, "Forever married to the backslider."

In Joel He is the Baptizer with the Holy Ghost and Fire

In Amos He is our Burden-Bearer

In Obadiah He is the Mighty to Save

In Jonah He is our great Foreign Missionary

In Micah He is the Messenger of Beautiful Feet

In Nahum He is the Avenger of God's Elect

In Habakkuk He is God's Evangelist, crying,
"Revive thy work in the midst of the years."

In Zephaniah He is our Savior

In Haggai He is the Restorer of God's lost
heritage

In Zechariah He is the Fountain opened to the
house of David for sin and uncleanness

In Malachi He is the Sun of Righteousness,
rising with healing in His wings

In Matthew He is the Messiah

In Mark He is the Wonder-Worker

In Luke He is the Son of Man

In John He is the Son of God

In Acts He is the Holy Ghost

In Romans He is our Justifier

In 1 and 2 Corinthians He is our Sanctifier

In Galatians He is our Redeemer from the
curse of the law

In Ephesians He is the Christ of unsearchable
riches

In Philippians He is the God who supplies all
our needs

In Colossians He is the fullness of the
Godhead, bodily

In 1 and 2 Thessalonians He is our Soon-
Coming King

In 1 and 2 Timothy He is our Mediator
between God and man

In Titus He is our Faithful Pastor

In Philemon He is a Friend that sticketh closer
than a brother

In Hebrews He is the Blood of the Everlasting
Covenant

In James He is our Great Physician, for "The
prayer of faith shall save the sick."

In 1 and 2 Peter He is our Chief Shepherd,
who soon shall appear with a crown of
unfading glory
In 1, 2 and 3 John He is Love
In Jude He is the Lord coming with ten
thousands of His saints
And in Revelation He is the King of kings and
Lord of lords!

He is Abel's Sacrifice, Noah's Rainbow, Abraham's Ram,
Isaac's Wells, Jacob's Ladder, Issachar's Burdens, Jacob's
Sceptre, Balaam's Shiloh, Moses' Rod, Joshua's Sun and
Moon that stood still, Elijah's Mantle, Elisha's Staff, Gideon's
Fleece, Samuel's Horn of Oil, David's Slingshot, Isaiah's Fig
Poultice, Hezekiah's Sundial, Daniel's Visions, Amos' Bur-
den, and Malachi's Sun of Righteousness.

He is Peter's Shadow, Stephen's Signs and Wonders,
Paul's Handkerchiefs and Aprons, and John's Pearly White
City.

He is Father to the Orphan, Husband to the Widow, to the
traveler in the night He is the Bright and Morning Star, to
those who walk in the Lonesome Valley He is the Lily of the
Valley, the Rose of Sharon, and Honey in the Rock.

He is the Brightness of God's Glory, the Express Image of
His Person, the King of Glory, the Pearl of Great Price, the
Rock in a Weary Land, the Cup that runneth over, the Rod
and Staff that comfort, and the Government of our life is
upon his shoulders.

He is Jesus of Nazareth, the Son of the living God! My
Savior, my Companion, my Lord and King!

—Author unknown

ANSWERS TO EASY TRIVIA QUESTIONS

1. How many men did Nebuchadnezzar see walking in the fiery furnace?
   A: Four—Daniel 3:25

2. What did Noah see in the sky?
   A: A rainbow—Genesis 9:11-17

3. "For whatsoever a man soweth, _____."
   A: That shall he also reap—Galatians 6:7

4. "But _____ found grace in the eyes of the Lord."
   A: Noah—Genesis 6:8

5. "Delilah said to _____, Tell me, I pray thee, wherein thy great strength lieth."
   A: Samson—Judges 16:6

6. "Pride goeth before destruction, and a haughty spirit before _____."
   A: A fall—Proverbs 16:18

7. "Follow me and I will make you _____."
   A: Fishers of men—Matthew 4:19

8. "Come unto me, all ye that labor and are _____."
   A: Heavy laden, and I will give you rest—Matthew 11:28

9. What were the names of the three disciples who were on the Mount of Transfiguration with Jesus?
   A: Peter, James, and John—Matthew 17:1

10. What was the name of the village that was known as the "City of David"?
    A: Bethlehem—Luke 2:4

11. Who was Andrew's brother?
    A: Peter—Matthew 10:2

12. "A soft answer turneth away _____."
    A: Wrath—Proverbs 15:1

13. The disciples were told to be wise as _____ and harmless as _____.
    A: Serpents, doves—Matthew 10:16

14. In what city did Joseph, Mary, and Jesus live?
    A: Nazareth—Matthew 2:23

15. What country did Joseph, Mary, and Jesus flee to?
    A: Egypt—Matthew 2:13

16. Where did the Wise Men come from?
    A: The east—Matthew 2:1

17. In the parable of the ten virgins, how many were wise and how many were foolish?
    A: Five wise and five foolish—Matthew 25:1,2

18. Where did Jesus perform His first miracle?
    A: Cana of Galilee—John 2:11

19. John the Baptist had an interesting diet of what?
    A: Locusts and wild honey—Matthew 3:1-4

20. In what book of the Bible do you find these words? "I am the living bread which came down from heaven; if any man eat of this bread, he shall live for ever."
    A: John—John 6:51

21. Peter said to Jesus, "Thou shalt never wash _____."
    a. My hands   b. My feet   c. My hair
    d. My clothes   e. My cup
    A: "B" or my feet—John 13:8

22. Who prayed three times a day at an open window?
    A: Daniel—Daniel 6:10

23. Who had an occupation as a tentmaker?
    A: Paul the apostle—Acts 18:1-3

24. Jesus was arrested in _____.
    A: The Garden of Gethsemane—Matthew 26:36

25. Who in the Bible could be called "The Lion Tamer"?
    A: Daniel—Daniel 6

26. John the Baptist was how much older than Jesus?
    A: About six months—Luke 1:24-27,36,56,57

27. Who in the Bible could carry the title "The Strong Man"?
    A: Samson—Judges 14-16

28. "If God be for us, _____?"
    A: Who can be against us—Romans 8:31

29. In what book of the Bible do you find the words, "There is no new thing under the sun"?
    A: Ecclesiastes—Ecclesiastes 1:9

30. According to the book of Proverbs, the beginning of knowledge is _____.
    A: Fear of the Lord—Proverbs 1:7

31. Who was the man who said, "Every kind of beasts, and of birds... hath been tamed by mankind"?
    A: James—James 3:7

32. In what book of the Bible do you find the story of the burning bush?
A: Exodus—Exodus 3:2-4

33. To whom did Jesus say, "Get thee behind me, Satan"?
A: Peter—Matthew 16:23

34. Who prayed inside of a fish?
A: Jonah—Jonah 2:1

35. What is the longest psalm in the Bible?
A: Psalm 119

36. The wise man built his house on _____ and the foolish man built his house on _____.
A: Rock, sand—Matthew 7:24-27

37. What was the name of the special food that God provided for the Children of Israel during the forty years in the wilderness?
A: Manna—Exodus 16:14,15

38. "I am _____ and _____, the beginning and the ending."
A: Alpha and Omega—Revelation 1:8

39. In what book of the Bible do you find the following words? "And there are also many other things which Jesus did, the which, if they should be written every one, I suppose that even the world itself could not contain the books that should be written."
A: John—John 21:25

40. Who in the Bible could carry the title "The Wise King"?
A: King Solomon—1 Kings 3-11

41. Bartimaeus was:
a. Lame   b. Deaf   c. Blind   d. Leprous
A: Blind—Mark 10:46

42. Who owned a coat that had many colors?
    A: Joseph—Genesis 37:3

43. "I am the true _____, and my Father is the husband-man."
    A: Vine—John 15:1

44. What Bible character was turned into a pillar of salt?
    A: Lot's wife—Genesis 19:15-26

45. What Bible character ate food that was given to the pigs?
    A: The prodigal son—Luke 15:11-16

46. What type of animal did Aaron fashion out of gold?
    A: A calf—Exodus 32:2-4

47. In what book in the Bible do you find the following words? "In my Father's house are many mansions."
    A: John—John 14:2

48. Who wrote with His finger on the ground?
    A: Jesus—John 8:6

49. Name the three gifts that the Wise Men from the East brought to Baby Jesus.
    A: Gold, frankincense, and myrrh—Matthew 2:11

50. "For what shall it profit a man, if he shall gain ____?"
    A: The whole world, and lose his own soul—Mark 8:36

51. How many books are in the New Testament?
    a. 23   b. 25   c. 27   d. 29
    A: "C" or 27

52. "Pray without _____."
    A: Ceasing—1 Thessalonians 5:17

53. Where in the Bible do you find the following words? "Behold, I stand at the door, and knock."
    A: Revelations—Revelation 3:20

54. Who said, "Silver or gold have I none, but such as I have give I thee"?

    A: Peter—Acts 3:6

55. What is the first lie recorded in the Bible?

    A: The serpent to Eve: "Ye shall not surely die"—Genesis 3:4

56. "I can do all things through _____."

    A: Christ which strengtheneth me—Philippians 4:13

57. How many books are in the Old Testament?

    a. 33   b. 35   b. 37   d. 39

    A: "D" or 39

58. The book of Hebrews tells us to entertain strangers because they might be _____.

    A: Angels—Hebrews 13:2

59. "Let the word of Christ dwell in you _____."

    A: Richly in all wisdom—Colossians 3:16

60. "Whatsoever ye do in word or deed, do all _____."

    A: In the name of Lord Jesus—Colossians 3:17

61. "The _____ of a good man are ordered by the Lord."

    A: Steps—Psalm 37:23

62. "I am the good _____."

    A: Shepherd—John 10:11

63. "Be not overcome of evil, but _____."

    A: Overcome evil with good—Romans 12:21

64. "I am the _____ of the _____."

    A: Light of the world—John 8:12

65. "I am the _____, the _____, and the _____."

    A: Way, truth, and life—John 14:6

66. "I am the _____; by me if any man enter in, he shall be saved."

A: Door—John 10:9

67. "If thy right eye offend thee, _____."

A: Pluck it out, and cast it from thee—Matthew 5:29

68. Who in the Bible was called, "A man after mine own heart"?

A: David—Acts 13:22

69. Who said, "Every son that is born ye shall cast into the river, and every daughter ye shall save alive"?

A: Pharaoh—Exodus 1:22

70. To whom was the following said? "Loose thy shoe from off thy foot; for the place whereon thou standest is holy."

A: To Joshua—Joshua 5:15; To Moses—Exodus 3:5

71. "_____, and it shall be given you; _____, and ye shall find: _____, and it will be opened unto you."

A: Ask, seek, knock—Matthew 7:7

72. Who said, "When I was a child, I spake as a child, I understood as a child, I thought as a child"?

A: Paul—1 Corinthians 13:11

73. Who said, "How can a man be born when he is old"?

A: Nicodemus—John 3:4

74. "For the wages of sin is death; _____."

A: But the gift of God is eternal life through Jesus Christ our Lord—Romans 6:23

75. Who said, "By their fruits ye shall know them"?

A: Jesus—Matthew 7:20

76. Who said, "Almost thou persuadest me to be a Christian"?

A: Agrippa—Acts 26:28

77. In what book in the Bible do you find the following? "So Joseph died, being a hundred and ten years old."
A: Genesis—Genesis 50:26

78. Who said, "Who touched my clothes?"
A: Jesus—Mark 5:30

79. To whom was the following spoken? "He was a murderer from the beginning, and abode not in the truth, because there is no truth in him."
A: Satan or the devil—John 8:44

80. What was the name of Abraham's wife?
A: Sarah—Genesis 17:18

81. In what book of the Bible do you find the laws concerning the eating of clean things?
A: Leviticus

82. In what book of the Bible do you find the phrase, "God is love"?
A: 1 John—1 John 4:8

83. "Thy word is a lamp unto my feet, and _____."
A: A light unto my path—Psalm 119:105

84. "For many are called, _____."
A: But few are chosen—Matthew 22:14

85. What is the shortest verse in the New Testament?
A: Jesus wept—John 11:35

86. "O death, where is thy sting? _____?"
A: O grave, where is thy victory?—1 Corinthians 15:55

87. How did Judas indicate to the crowd who Jesus was?
A: By kissing him—Matthew 26:47-49

88. Who in the Bible could be called "Mr. Patience"?
A: Job—Job 1–42

89. To whom were the following words spoken? "Because thou has done this, thou are cursed."
   A: To the serpent—Genesis 3:14

90. David's occupation before he became a king was ___.
   A: A shepherd—1 Samuel 16:11-13

91. "And ye shall know the truth, and the truth shall ___."
   A: Make you free—John 8:32

92. What is greater than faith and hope?
   A: Charity (KJV) or love (NIV)—1 Corinthian 13:13

93. What happens when the blind lead the blind?
   A: Both shall fall into the ditch—Matthew 15:14

94. To whom was the following comment made? "For God so loved the world, that he gave his only begotten Son, that whosoever believeth in him should not perish, but have everlasting life."
   A: Nicodemus—John 3:9-16

95. "For where two or three are gathered together in my name, _____."
   A: There am I in the midst of them—Matthew 18:20

96. In what book of the Bible do you find the following words? "Let everything that hath breath praise the Lord."
   A: Psalms—Psalm 150:6

97. Cain did what for a living?
   A: He was a tiller of the ground—Genesis 4:2

98. Peter did what for a living?
   A: He was a fisherman—Matthew 4:18

99. Which apostle was called Doubting _____?
   A: Thomas—John 20:24-29

100. Abel did what for a living?

    A: He was a keeper of sheep—Genesis 4:2

101. Joseph, the husband of Mary, did what for a living?

    A: He was a carpenter—Matthew 13:55

102. In what book of the Bible do you find the words, "Blessed is the man that walketh not in the counsel of the ungodly"?

    A: Psalms—Psalm 1

103. "Speak; for thy servant _____."

    A: Heareth—1 Samuel 3:10

104. In what book of the Bible do you find the words, "In the beginning was the Word and the Word was with God, and the Word was God"?

    A: John—John 1:1

105. "The Lord is my strength and _____."

    A: My shield—Psalm 28:7; my song—Exodus 15:2

106. Who said that even all the hairs on our head are numbered by God?

    A: Jesus—Matthew 10:30

107. Paul told Timothy to take something for his stomach's sake. What was it?

    A: A little wine—1 Timothy 5:23

108. "Greater love hath no man than this, _____."

    A: That a man lay down his life for his friends—John 15:13

109. When did Jesus make more than a hundred gallons of very good wine?

    A: At the Cana wedding—John 2:1-11

110. Who made clothes out of leaves that were sewed together?

    A: Adam and Eve—Genesis 3:7

111. Who was the wife of Boaz?
     A: Ruth—Ruth 4:13

112. Who in the Bible could be called "The Giant Killer"?
     A: David—1 Samuel 17

113. Who was the oldest brother—Cain or Abel?
     A: Cain—Genesis 4:1,2

114. Who gave Jesus some food to help feed the 5000?
     A: A lad—John 6:9

115. Who said, "My soul doth magnify the Lord... he hath
     regarded the low estate of his handmaiden... gener-
     ations shall call me blessed"?
     A: Mary—Luke 1:46-48

116. Who said that, "I have fought a good fight, I have
     finished my course, I have kept the faith"?
     A: Paul—2 Timothy 4:7

117. What was the name of the man who gave each man in
     his army of 300 a trumpet and an empty pitcher?
     A: Gideon—Judges 7:15,16

118. Who took golden earrings and made them into a calf?
     A: Aaron—Exodus 32:2-4

119. Jesus said, "Peace, be still." Who was He addressing?
     A: He spoke to the stormy waters—Mark 4:37-39

120. "Saul hath slain his thousands, and David his ____."
     A: Ten thousands—1 Samuel 18:7,8

121. What was Paul's other name?
     A: Saul—Acts 13:9

122. Jesus mixed something with clay and put it on the eyes
     of the blind man to make him see. What did Jesus mix
     with the clay?
     A: Spittle—John 9:6

123. When the Roman soldiers pierced Jesus in the side
     with a spear, what came out?
     A: Water and blood—John 19:34

124. "For what is a man profited, if he shall gain the whole
     world, and lose his own _____."
     A: Soul—Matthew 16:26

125. Did Judas Iscariot keep the betrayal money or did he
     give it back?
     A: He gave it back—Matthew 27:3-5

126. The Spirit of God descended on Jesus in the form of a

     _____.

     A: Dove—Matthew 3:16

127. "For the law was given by Moses, but grace and
     _____ came by Jesus Christ."
     A: Truth—John 1:17

128. What did Ananias sell in order to get money to give to
     the apostles?
     A: Land—Acts 5:1-3

129. Who said, "No prophet is accepted in his own country"?
     A: Jesus—Luke 4:24

130. Water was in how many pots that Jesus turned into
     wine?
     A: Six—John 2:6

131. Who was Jesus talking about when he said, "I have not
     found so great a faith, no, not in Israel"?
     A: The centurion—Luke 7:2-10

132. "Go ye therefore, and teach all nations, baptizing them
     _____."

     A: In the name of the Father, and of the Son, and of the
     Holy Ghost—Matthew 28:19

133. "Judge not, _____."
    A: That ye be not judged—Matthew 7:1

134. Who brought back to life the son of the widow in whose house he was staying?
    A: Elijah—1 Kings 17:17-22

135. What was the name of the garden Jesus prayed in?
    A: Gethsemane—Matthew 26:36

136. In what book of the Bible do we read about God's armor?
    A: Ephesians 6

137. "Without the _____ _____ _____ there is no forgiveness" (NIV).
    A: Shedding of blood—Hebrews 9:22

138. How many demons did Mary Magdalene have in her?
    a. Two   b. Three   c. Five
    d. Seven   e. Nine
    A: "D" or seven—Luke 8:2

139. How old was the daughter of Jairus?
    A: About 12—Luke 8:42

140. What book comes before 1 Kings?
    A: 2 Samuel

141. What are the names of the two men who had a sharp argument over John Mark?
    A: Paul and Barnabas—Acts 15:39

142. Which chapter in the Bible lists the heroes of faith?
    A: Hebrews 11

143. What Bible character stood on Mars Hill?
    A: Paul—Acts 17:22

144. "With God all things are _____."
    A: Possible—Matthew 19:26

145. A man who has his quiver full of them is happy. What is
     in the quiver?
     A: Children (KJV) or sons (NIV)—Psalms 127:4,5

146. Who was the first person to experience fear in the
     Bible?
     A: Adam—Genesis 3:9,10

147. "_____ _____ is the same yesterday and today and
     forever" (NIV).
     A: Jesus Christ—Hebrews 13:8

148. Peter says that in the last days _____ will come.
     A: Scoffers—2 Peter 3:3

149. Who shut the door on Noah's Ark?
     A: The Lord—Genesis 7:16

150. What time of day did Adam and Eve hear God walking
     in the Garden of Eden?
     A: In the cool of the day—Genesis 3:8

151. Who said, "I will exalt my throne above the stars of
     God"?
     A: Lucifer—Isaiah 14:13

152. What Bible character talks about "the twinkling of an
     eye"?
     A: Paul—1 Corinthians 15:52; 1:1,2

153. Who was the first person in the Bible to take a nap?
     A: Adam—Genesis 2:20,21

154. Paul prayed _____ times to have his thorn in the flesh
     removed.
     A: Three—2 Corinthians 12:7,8

155. Quote Romans 3:23.
     A: "For all have sinned, and come short of the glory of
     God"

156. What Bible character said, "Where your treasure is,
there will your heart be also"?
A: Jesus—Luke 12:34

157. What is the book just before Micah?
A: Jonah

158. Into how many pieces was Jesus' seamless garment
cut?
A: It was not cut—John 19:23,24

159. In what book of the Bible does it talk about 100-pound
(or a talent) hailstones?
A: Revelation—Revelation 16:21

160. Who had a spear with the iron head weighing 600
shekels?
A: Goliath—1 Samuel 17:4,7

161. In what chapter of the Bible do we find Jesus' high
priestly prayer?
A: John 17

162. The Egyptians thought Sarah was related to Abraham
in what way?
A: They thought she was his sister—Genesis 12:19

163. Which tribe of Israel had the responsibility of moving
the tabernacle?
A: Levi—Numbers 1:51

164. What book comes after the book of Obadiah?
A: Jonah

165. What is the first word in the Bible?
A: In—Genesis 1:1

166. In what chapter of the Bible do you find the phrase,
"He leadeth me beside the still waters"?
A: Psalm 23—Psalm 23:2

167. God told Adam and Eve not to eat what kind of fruit?
A: The Bible does not say

168. "_____ goeth before destruction, and a haughty spirit before a fall."
A: Pride—Proverbs 16:18

169. When Jesus was 12 He was unintentionally left behind by Mary and Joseph. How many days did they look for Him?
A: Three—Luke 2:46

170. How many times a year did the high priest enter the Holy of Holies to make atonement for all the sins of Israel?
A: Once a year—Leviticus 16:34

171. Who said, "Naked I came from my mother's womb" (NIV).
A: Job—Job 1:21,22

172. How old was Jesus when it was first mentioned that He went to Jerusalem for the Passover?
A: Twelve—Luke 2:42

173. How many men believed in Christ after Peter's second sermon?
A: About 5000—Acts 4:4

174. "For the wages of sin is _____, but the gift of God is _____ _____" (NIV).
A: Death, eternal life—Romans 6:23

175. Two Old Testament cities were destroyed because of their great wickedness. What were their names?
A: Sodom and Gomorrah—Genesis 19:28,29

176. In the Garden of Gethsemane, Jesus sweat great drops of _____
A: Blood—Luke 22:44

177. The Bible suggests that a thousand years in God's sight is as how long?

A: A day—Psalm 90:4

178. Who said, "Foxes have holes and birds of the air have nests" (NIV)?

A: Jesus—Matthew 8:20

179. Which of the 12 disciples was in charge of the money?

A: Judas Iscariot—John 12:4-6

180. What book comes before the book of Lamentations?

A: Jeremiah

181. Who said, "Before Abraham was born, I am" (NIV)?

A: Jesus—John 8:58

182. In what book of the Bible do we find the quotation, "God helps those who help themselves"?

A: It is not in the Bible

183. What is the name of the disciple who took care of Jesus mother after His death?

A: John, the disciple whom Jesus loved—John 19:26, 27

184. Quote Philippians 4:4.

A: "Rejoice in the Lord always. I will say it again: Rejoice!" (NIV)

185. What book comes before the book of Isaiah?

A: Song of Solomon (KJV); Song of Songs (NIV)

186. What Bible character said, "What must I do to be saved?"

A: The jailer—Acts 16:27,29,30

187. How many chapters are there in the book of Jude?

A: One

188. Who asked Jesus, "Are you the king of the Jews?" (NIV).

    A: Pilate—John 18:33

189. "Trust in the Lord with all thine _____; and lean not unto thine own _____."

    A: Heart, understanding—Proverbs 3:5

190. When the Philistines finally captured Samson, what did they do to him?

    A: Gouged out his eyes—Judges 16:20,21

191. What was the first thing that Adam and Eve did after they sinned?

    A: Sewed fig leaves together "to cover themselves"— Genesis 3:6,7

192. "For nothing is _____ with God" (NIV).

    A: Impossible—Luke 1:37

193. What are the names of the two Bible characters who did not die?

    A: Enoch and Elijah—Genesis 5:24; 2 Kings 2:11

194. "For by grace are ye _____ through _____; and that not of yourselves: it is the gift of God."

    A: Saved, faith—Ephesians 2:8

195. Peter suggests that the day of the Lord will come as a
    _____.

    A: Thief—2 Peter 3:10

196. What Bible character said, "I am a man of unclean lips"?

    A: Isaiah—Isaiah 6:5

197. What chapter of the Bible is considered the love chapter?

    A: 1 Corinthians 13

198. "The _____ says in his heart, 'There is no _____.' "
(NIV).

A: Fool, God—Psalm 14:1

199. On the seventh day of creation, what did God do?

A: Rest—Genesis 2:3

200. Who told the first lie in the Bible?

A: The serpent—Genesis 3:4,5

201. When Jesus healed the ten lepers, how many returned and thanked Him?

A: One—Luke 17:15

202. How many days did it take Nehemiah to inspect the city walls of Jerusalem before rebuilding them?

A: Three—Nehemiah 2:11-13

203. Quote John 1:12.

A: "But as many as receive him, to them gave he the power to become the sons of God, even to them that believe on his name."

204. What was the hometown of King David?

A: Bethlehem—1 Samuel 17:12

205. What book comes after the book of Malachi?

A: Matthew

206. John wrote the book of Revelation on what island?

A: Patmos—Revelation 1:9-11

207. How many chapters are there in the book of Colossians?

A: Four

208. In what book of the Bible do we find the words, "Abstain from all appearance of evil"?

A: 1 Thessalonians 5:22

209. On what mountain did Noah's Ark come to rest?
    A: Ararat—Genesis 8:4

210. What are the names of the two men who wrapped Jesus' body for burial?
    A: Joseph of Arimathea and Nicodemus—John 19:38-40

211. The poor widow in the book of Luke put how many coins into the temple treasury?
    A: Two—Luke 21:2

212. In what book of the Bible do we find the phrase, "The very hairs of your head are all numbered"?
    A: Matthew—Matthew 10:30

213. Who is the author of the book of Zephaniah?
    A: Zephaniah—Zephaniah 1:1

214. Who was the first person to enter the empty tomb of Jesus?
    A: Peter—John 20:4-6

215. Isaiah compares our righteousness to _____ _____.
    A: Filthy rags—Isaiah 64:6

216. What is the number of the beast in the book of Revelation?
    A: Six hundred sixty-six—Revelation 13:18

217. In what book of the Bible do we find the phrase, "Give us this day our daily bread"?
    A: Matthew—Matthew 6:11

218. Who succeeded Moses as leader of the children of Israel?
    A: Joshua—Numbers 27:18-23

219. In what book of the Bible do we find the words, "Without the shedding of blood there is no forgiveness" (NIV)?

    A: Hebrews—Hebrews 9:22

220. Who disguises himself as an angel of light?

    A: Satan—2 Corinthians 11:14

221. When David was a boy, what two fierce animals did he kill?

    A: A lion and a bear—1 Samuel 17:36,37

222. How many years will Satan be bound in the Abyss (bottomless pit)?

    A: One thousand—Revelation 20:2,3

223. What was the name of the type of leaf that Adam and Eve wore before the fall?

    A: They wore nothing before the fall—Genesis 2:25

224. What Bible character originally said, "It is more blessed to give than to receive" (NIV)?

    A: Jesus—Acts 20:35

225. Name the first five people mentioned in the Bible.

    A: Adam, Eve, Cain, Abel, Enoch—Genesis 2:19,20; 3:20; 4:1,2,17

226. How many of the sacrifice sheep did Moses take into the Ark with him?

    A: Moses was not on the Ark

227. Lydia is known for selling what?

    A: Purple cloth—Acts 16:14

228. What does the Bible say has never been tamed by man?

    A: The human tongue—James 3:8

229. The Bible says there is one thing that never fails. What is it?

A: Love—1 Corinthians 13:8 (NIV)

230. In what book of the Bible do we find the words, "For my yoke is easy and my burden is light"?

A: Matthew—Matthew 11:30

231. How many times is the word Bible used in the Bible?

A: None

232. What book comes after the book of Micah?

A: Nahum

233. "For where your _____ is, there your _____ will be also" (NIV).

A: Treasure, heart—Luke 12:34

234. What book comes after the book of Hebrews?

A: James

235. On what two parts of the body will the mark of the beast be placed?

A: Forehead or right hand—Revelation 13:16

236. In what book of the Bible do you find the words born again?

A: John—John 3:3

237. In what book of the Bible is the verse, "Cleanliness is next to godliness"?

A: It is not in the Bible

238. Jonah purchased his boat ticket in what city?

A: Joppa—Jonah 1:3

239. "I can do all things through _____ who _____ me."

A: Christ, strengtheneth—Philippians 4:13

240. What are the names of the three disciples who were the shortest distance from Jesus in Gethsemane while He prayed?

    A: Peter, James, John—Matthew 26:37

241. In what book of the Bible do we find the words, "If any of you lack wisdom, let him ask of God"?

    A: James—James 1:5

242. What is the name of the disciple who was instructed to touch the nail prints in Jesus' hands after His resurrection?

    A: Thomas—John 20:25-27

243. What was the name of the angel who spoke to Mary the mother of Jesus?

    A: Gabriel—Luke 1:26,27

244. Judas agreed to betray for how many pieces of silver?

    A: Thirty—Matthew 26:14,15

245. What Bible character said, "How can a man be born when he is old?"

    A: Nicodemus—John 3:4

246. Who does the Bible say holds the keys of hell and death?

    A: Jesus—Revelation 1:18

247. What were the names of the two sisters of Lazarus?

    A: Mary and Martha—John 11:1,2

248. What kind of valley is described in Psalm 23?

    A: The valley of the shadow of death—Psalm 23:4

249. What Bible character put out a fleece to test God?

    A: Gideon—Judges 6:36,37

ANSWERS TO FAIRLY EASY TRIVIA QUESTIONS

1. What was the name of the prophet who was very hairy and wore a leather belt?
   A: Elijah—2 Kings 1:8

2. What is the name of the man who King David arranged to have killed because he wanted his wife?
   A: Uriah—2 Samuel 11:2-17

3. The earth, seas, grass, herb yielding seed, and the tree yielding fruit were created on which day of creation?
   a. 2nd   b. 3rd   c. 4th   d. 5th
   A: "B" or third—Genesis 1:10-13

4. What was the name of the man who inherited Elijah's mantle?
   A: Elisha—2 Kings 2:12,13

5. What was the name of the man who owned a seamless coat?
   A: Jesus—John 19:23

6. What was the name of the man who worked seven years to earn a wife?
   A: Jacob—Genesis 29:20

7. What Bible prophet said, "Behold, a virgin shall conceive, and bear a son, and shall call his name Immanuel"?
   A: Isaiah—Isaiah 7:14

8. How old was Joseph when he was given his coat of many colors?

   A: 17—Genesis 37:2,3

9. What was the name of the high priest's servant who had his ear cut off by the Apostle Peter?

   A: Malchus—John 18:10

10. What was the name of the Bible character who was blind and killed 3000 people while at a religious feast?

    A: Samson—Judges 16:23, 27-30

11. What was the name of the Jewish man who called himself greater than King Solomon?

    A: Jesus—Matthew 12:42

12. After David knocked Goliath to the ground with a stone from his sling, he cut off Goliath's head with his own sword. True or false?

    A: False. David cut off Goliath's head with Goliath's own sword—1 Samuel 17:50,51

13. What nation of people got sick and tired of eating quail for dinner?

    A: The nation of Israel—Numbers 11:32,33

14. Which came first—the plague of lice or the plague of frogs?

    A: The plague of frogs—Exodus 8:1-18

15. What was the name of the Bible prophet who was fed by birds?

    A: Elijah—1 Kings 17:1-6

16. About whom was the following statement made? "Among those that are born of women there is not a greater prophet than..."?

    A: John the Baptist—Luke 7:28

17. On what mountain did Noah's Ark come to rest?

    A: Ararat—Genesis 8:4

18. What was the name of the queen who came from a far country to witness for herself the wisdom of King Solomon?

    A: The Queen of Sheba—1 Kings 10:1-10

19. What was the name of the man who wore clothes made out of camel's hair?

    A: John the Baptist—Matthew: 3:1,4

20. At whose command were 300 pitchers broken?

    A: Gideon—Judges 7:16,19

21. How many days was Saul blind while in Damascus?

    A: Three—Acts 9:8,9

22. Who were the people who found frogs on their beds and in their ovens?

    A: The Egyptians—Exodus 8:3,6

23. Who said, "Divide the living child in two, and give half to the one, and half to the other"?

    A: Solomon—1 Kings 3:15,25

24. What was the name of the Bible character who was a cupbearer to a king and also an engineer?

    A: Nehemiah—Nehemiah 1:11; 2:5

25. What was the name of the man who came to Jesus by night to talk with him?

    A: Nicodemus—John 3:1,2

26. How old was Methuselah when he died?

    A: 969 years old—Genesis 5:27

27. Name the fruit of the Spirit.

    A: Love, joy, peace. longsuffering, gentleness, goodness, faith, meekness, temperance (self-control)—Galatians 5:22,23

28. How many windows were in Noah's Ark?

    A: One—Genesis 6:16

29. What was the name of the man who was released from prison by an angel?

    A: Peter—Acts 12:5-11

30. In what book of the Bible do you find the words, "Of making many books there is no end"?

    A: Ecclesiastes—Ecclesiastes 12:12

31. What were the names of the two disciples who were called "The Sons of Thunder"?

    A: James and John—Mark 3:17

32. In order to see Jesus more clearly, Zacchaeus climbed what type of tree?

    A: A sycamore tree—Luke 19:2-4

33. What was the name of the man who escaped from Damascus in a basket?

    A: Saul (Paul)—Acts 9:23-25

34. How many people were saved in Noah's Ark?

    A: Eight—Genesis 6:10,18

35. What was the name of the man who issued the decree that all the world should be taxed?

    A: Caesar Augustus—Luke 2:1

36. What was the name of the tree that Adam and Eve were told not to eat fruit from?

    A: The tree of knowledge of good and evil—Genesis 2:17

37. What was the name of the man who foretold of the seven good years and the seven lean years in Egypt?

    A: Joseph—Genesis 41:15,25,29,30

38. What was the name of the first woman judge in Israel?

    A: Deborah—Judges 4:4

39. What was the name of the couple who died because they lied to the Holy Spirit?

    A: Ananias and Sapphira—Acts 5:1-10

40. Who was accused of eating in the cornfields on the Sabbath?

    A: Jesus—Luke 6:1,2

41. The Israelites were bitten by _____ and were healed by looking at the same creature made out of brass.

    A: Serpents—Numbers 21:9

42. Moses had a brother. What was his name?

    A: Aaron—Exodus 7:1

43. How many times did Samuel go to Eli the priest, thinking that Eli had called him?

    A: Three times—1 Samuel 3:4-8

44. What was the name of the queen who was devoured by dogs?

    A: Jezebel—1 Kings 16:30-31; 2 Kings 9:36

45. How old was Joseph when his brothers sold him into slavery?

    A: 17—Genesis 37:2,28

46. What is the name of the angel who told Mary that she would be the mother of Jesus?

    A: Gabriel—Luke 1:26

47. How many years did the children of Israel eat manna?

    A: Forty years—Exodus 16:35

48. How many years did God give Noah to build the Ark?

    A: 120 years—Genesis 6:3

49. How many stories or levels were in the Ark?

    A: Three—Genesis 6:16

50. What was the name of the father who was struck dumb, because of unbelief, until his son was born?

A: Zacharias—Luke 1:13,18,20

51. What was the name of the man who had to work many years and got two wives as a result?

A: Jacob—Genesis 29:16-28

52. What was in the Ark in the Tabernacle?

A: The Ten Commandments, Aaron's Rod, and a pot of manna—Hebrews 9:4

53. The Bible talks of a very tiny seed that becomes a very large tree. What is the name of the seed?

A: Mustard—Matthew 13:31,32

54. How many Marys are mentioned in the Bible?

A: Six—Mary the mother of Jesus—Matthew 2:11 and many passages; Mary Magdalene—Matthew 27:56 and many passages; Mary the mother of James and Joses—Matthew 27:56; Mary the sister of Martha—John 11:1,2; Mary the wife of Cleophas—John 19:25; and the Mary Paul greeted in Romans 16:6

55. What was the name of the woman who was called "The Seller of Purple"?

A: Lydia—Acts 16;14

56. What is the last line of the Twenty-third Psalm?

A: And I will dwell in the house of the Lord for ever—Psalm 23:6

57. Jesus said that He would rebuild the temple in how many days?

A: Three—John 2:19

58. The manger is to Jesus as the basket in the bulrushes is to _____.

A: Moses—Exodus 2:3,10

59. Who said, "Repent ye: for the kingdom of heaven is at hand"?

A: John the Baptist—Matthew 3:1-2

60. On what mountain did Moses receive the law?

A: Sinai—Exodus 24:12-16

61. Who replaced Moses as the leader of the children of Israel?

A: Joshua—Joshua 1:1-9

62. To whom was the following statement made? "Take nothing for your journey, neither staves, nor scrip, neither bread, neither money; neither have two coats apiece."

A: The twelve disciples—Luke 9:1-3

63. Timotheus' mother was a Jewess and his father _____.

A: Greek—Acts 16:1

64. What color was Esau's complexion?

a. Pale   b. Light brown   c. Red
d. Black   e. White

A: "C" or red—Genesis 25:25

65. What color was the robe that Jesus wore when the soldiers taunted Him?

A: Purple—John 19:2

66. Genesis is to Malachi as Matthew is to _____.

A: Revelation (first book to last in Old Testament; first book to last in New Testament)

67. Matthew, Mark, and John called it Golgotha or the place of the skull. What did Luke call it?

A: Calvary—Luke 23:33

68. In what book of the Bible do you find the words, "Make haste, my beloved, and be thou like to a roe or to a young hart upon the mountains of spices"?

A: Song of Solomon—Song of Solomon 8:14

69. In what book of the Bible do you find the words, "Be strong and of a good courage"?
    a. Job   b. Philippians   c. Joshua
    d. Ephesians
    A: "C" or Joshua—Joshua 1:6,9

70. Who said, "I am innocent of the blood of this just person"?
    A: Pilate—Matthew 27:24

71. How many hours was Jesus on the cross?
    A: Six—Mark 15:25,34-37

72. What was the relationship of Zebedee to James and John?
    A: Father—Matthew 4:21

73. In what book of the Bible do you find the words, "Blessed are the meek: for they shall inherit the earth"?
    A: Matthew—Matthew 5:5

74. In what book of the Bible do you find the Ten Commandments?
    A: Exodus—Exodus 20:3-17

75. Who said, "He was oppressed, and he was afflicted, yet he opened not his mouth"?
    a. Isaiah   b. Jeremiah   c. Ezekiel
    d. Hosea
    A: "A" or Isaiah—Isaiah 53:7

76. Who was born first—Jacob or Esau?
    A: Esau—Genesis 25:25,26

77. The spies who spied out the land of Canaan said that it flowed with _____ and _____.
    A: Milk and honey—Numbers 13:27

78. Who was stoned to death for preaching that Jesus was the savior?
    A: Stephen—Acts 7:55-60

79. "It is easier for a _____ to go through the eye of a _____, than for a _____ to enter into the kingdom of God."

    A: Camel, needle, rich man—Matthew 19:24

80. In the parable of the ten virgins, five of them were wise and five were foolish. Why were the foolish ones foolish?

    A: They brought no oil for their lamps—Matthew 25:1-3

81. Who were the disciples who argued about sitting on the right and left hand side of Jesus?

    A: James and John—Matthew 10:2; 20:20-24

82. Who witnessed the conversation between Moses, Elijah, and Jesus?

    A: Peter, James, and John—Matthew 17:1-3

83. On what day of creation were the sun, the moon, and the stars created?

    A: The fourth day—Genesis 1:14-19

84. Paul and Barnabas had an argument over a certain man traveling with them on their missionary journey. What was the man's name?

    A: John Mark—Acts 15:37-39

85. What were the names of the two spies who spied Canaan Land and gave a favorable report?

    A: Joshua and Caleb—Numbers 14:6-9

86. What Bible character was renamed Israel?

    A: Jacob—Genesis 32:28

87. What preacher was mad because his preaching caused a whole city to repent?

    A: Jonah—Jonah 3:1-5; 4:1

88. On what day of creation were the sea creatures and fowl created?

    A: The fifth day—Genesis 1:20-23

89. Who saw Satan fall from heaven?
    A: Jesus—Luke 10:17,18

90. Who had a wrestling match with God and won?
    A: Jacob—Genesis 32:24-30

91. Which came first,"Thou shalt not kill" or "Thou shalt not steal"?
    A: Thou shalt not kill—Exodus 20:13,15

92. What was the name of the apostle who was shipwrecked three different times?
    A: Paul—2 Corinthians 11:25

93. On which day of creation were the land animals and man created?
    A: The sixth day—Genesis 1:24-31

94. What Bible character had 300 concubines?
    A: King Solomon—1 Kings 11:1,3

95. What was the name of a physician in the Bible who was also an author?
    A: Dr. Luke—Colossians 4:14

96. Who sold their younger brother into slavery?
    A: The brothers of Joseph—Genesis 37:26-28

97. Lot escaped from the city of Sodom with whom?
    A: His two daughters—Genesis 19:30

98. What was the name of the man who ordered the execution of 450 priests?
    A: Elijah—1 Kings 18:22,40

99. Which book in the Bible was written to an "Elect Lady"?
    A: 2 John—2 John 1:1

100. Jesus said that it was proper to pay tribute (money) to what man?
     A: Caesar—Mark 12:14-17

101. Simon Peter cut off the ear of the high priest's servant. Which ear did he cut off?

A: Right ear—John 18:10

102. What Bible character said, " A little leaven leaveneth the whole lump"?

A: Paul—1 Corinthians 5:6; Galatians 5:9

103. How many years did Jacob work for his Uncle Laban in payment for his daughters?

A: Fourteen—Genesis 29:18-28

104. Who was healed—the son or the daughter of Jairus?

A: The daughter—Mark 5:22,23,35-42

105. "Blessed are the pure in heart: _____."

A: For they shall see God—Matthew 5:8

106. What book in the Bible has a threat against anyone adding to it or taking away from it?

A: Revelation—Revelation 22:18,19

107. What was the name of the man who lifted up the infant Jesus at the temple and praised God?

A: Simeon—Luke 2:25-31

108. In what book in the Bible do you find the following: "For the Lord himself shall descend from heaven with a shout, with the voice of the archangel"?

A: 1 Thessalonians 4:16,17

109. What sign was given to the shepherds at the time of Christ's birth?

A: A babe wrapped in swaddling clothes, lying in a manger—Luke 2:8,12

110. How many loaves and how many fishes did Jesus use to feed the 5000?

A: Five loaves and two fishes—Matthew 14:17-21

111. For what reason did the rich young ruler come to
     Christ?
     A: For eternal life—Matthew 19:16

112. What does the name Emmanuel mean?
     A: God with us—Matthew 1:23

113. What was the name of the king who sought to take the
     life of the Baby Jesus?
     A: Herod—Matthew 2:13

114. What was the name of the criminal who was released in
     place of Jesus?
     A: Barabbas—Luke 23:18

115. What was the name of the mother of Abraham's first
     son?
     A: Hagar—Genesis 16:15

116. What Bible character had a dream that his parents and
     brothers would bow down before him?
     A: Joseph—Genesis 37:5-7

117. The city walls of _____ fell down when the trumpets
     were blown.
     A: Jericho—Joshua 6:2-5

118. Name the two bodies of water that the children of Israel
     crossed on dry ground.
     A: The Red Sea and the Jordan River—Exodus 13;18;
        Joshua 1:2

119. Where in the Bible do you find the longest recorded
     prayer of Jesus?
     A: John—John 17

120. What was Matthew's other name?
     A: Levi—Mark 2:14, Luke 5:27

121. What is the first beatitude?

    A: Blessed are the poor in spirit: for theirs is the king-
    dom of heaven—Matthew 5:3

122. Is Bethlehem located in Galilee or in Judea?

    A: Judea—Matthew 2:1

123. Jesus said that there were two masters you could not
    serve at the same time. What were they?

    A: God and mammon—Matthew 6:24

124. What was Sarah's other name?

    A: Sarai—Genesis 17:15

125. Who said, "Am I my brother's keeper?"

    A: Cain—Genesis 4:9

126. Who said, "The Lord gave, and the Lord hath taken
    away; blessed be the name of the Lord"?

    A: Job—Job 1:21

127. Who owned a coat that was dipped in blood?

    A: Joseph—Genesis 37:31

128. Who was bitten by a snake and shook it off into a fire
    and felt no harm?

    A: Paul—Acts 28:3-5

129. Peter was told by Jesus to forgive his brother how many
    times?

    A: Seventy times seven (490) times—Matthew 18:21,
    22

130. Who was the first Bible character to use a riddle?

    A: Samson—Judges 14:12

131. What was the New Testament word for teacher?

    A: Rabbi or Master—John 1:38

132. What is the name of the man who carried Jesus' cross?

    A: Simon of Cyrene—Matthew 27:32

133. In order for a man to become a bond slave, what did he have to do?
     A: Have his ear pierced—Exodus 21:5,6

134. In speaking of Jesus, who said, "Certainly this was a righteous man"?
     A: The centurion—Luke 23:46,47

135. How many men did Nebuchadnezzar see walking in the fiery furnace?
     A: Four—Daniel 3:24,25

136. In what book of the Bile do we read the words, "Whoso findeth a wife findeth a good thing"?
     A: Proverbs—Proverbs 18:22

137. What was the name of the Bible character who put a veil over his face to hide the glory of God?
     A: Moses—2 Corinthians 3:7,13

138. Jesus was a descendant of what tribe of Israel?
     A: Judah—Hebrews 7:14

139. Saul had a troubled spirit that could only be soothed by
     _____.
     A: Music—1 Samuel 16:15,16

140. The disciples were first called Christians in what city?
     A: Antioch—Acts 11:26

141. What book comes before the book of Joel?
     A: Hosea

142. Who prayed the shortest prayer recorded in the Bible?
     A: Peter—Matthew 14:29,30

143. Quote the shortest prayer in the Bible.
     A: "Lord, save me!"—Matthew 14:30

144. What Bible character said, "What a wretched man I am" (NIV)?

    A: Paul the apostle—Romans 7:24

145. What man in the Bible was called the Son of Encouragement (or consolation)?

    A: Barnabas—Acts 4:36

146. Quote Isaiah 53:6.

    A: "All we like sheep have gone astray; we have turned everyone to his own way; and the Lord hath laid on him the iniquity of us all"

147. In what book of the Bible do we read the words, "Your attitude should be the same as that of Christ Jesus" (NIV)?

    A: Philippians—Philippians 2:5

148. "Believe on the Lord Jesus Christ, and thou shalt be _____, and thy _____."

    A: Saved, house—Acts 16:31

149. In what book of the Bible do we read the words, "Whatsoever a man soweth, that shall he also reap"?

    A: Galatians—Galatians 6:7

150. What does Proverbs 22 suggest is more desirable than great riches?

    A: A good name—Proverbs 22:1

151. What is the name of the first Bible character mentioned drinking wine?

    A: Noah—Genesis 9:20,21

152. What is the number of the largest group of people to whom Christ appeared after His resurrection?

    A: More than 500—1 Corinthians 15:6

153. Name the three Bible characters who are mentioned as fasting for 40 days.
     A: Moses, Elijah, Jesus—Exodus 34:27,28; 1 Kings 19:2,8; Matthew 4:1,2

154. List the books of the Bible that are named after women.
     A: Esther and Ruth

155. Quote Philippians 1:21.
     A: "For to me to live is Christ and to die is gain."

156. If a man hates his son, he will not bother to do what?
     A: Spank him—Proverbs 13:24

157. Which book comes before the book of Obadiah?
     A: Amos

158. What Bible character said, "Here am I; send me"?
     A: Isaiah—Isaiah 6:8

159. The country of Lebanon is famous for what kind of trees?
     A: Cedar—Psalm 104:16

160. _____ was called God's friend.
     A: Abraham—James 2:23

161. According to Timothy, what will people love in the last days?
     A: Themselves, money, and pleasure (NIV); Their own-selves, pleasures (KJV)—2 Timothy 3:1-5

162. At the time of Christ's birth, who issued a decree for a census (NIV) or tax (KJV)?
     A: Caesar Augustus—Luke 2:1

163. In what book of the Bible do we find the words, "Every man did that which was right in his own eyes"?
     A: Judges—Judges 17:6

164. What book comes after the book of Habakkuk?

A: Zephaniah

165. How many days after Jesus' resurrection did He ascend to heaven?

A: Forty—Acts 1:3,9

166. What Bible character called her husband master (lord)?

A: Sarah—1 Peter 3:6

167. Name the Bible character who was buried by God.

A: Moses—Deuteronomy 34:5,6

168. According to 2 Timothy, Scripture is profitable for four things. What are they?

A: Doctrine, reproof, correction, and instruction in righteousness (KJV); teaching, rebuking, correcting, and training in righteousness (NIV)—2 Timothy 3:16

169. What was the name of the father of James and John?

A: Zebedee—Matthew 4:21

170. Did Hezekiah author the book of Hezekiah?

A: There is no book of Hezekiah

171. Jesus told His disciples in the book of Acts that they would be witnesses in three specific locations. What were those locations?

A: Jerusalem, Judea, Samaria—Acts 1:8

172. What did the rich man in hell want?

A: Water—Luke 16:22-24

173. Quote 1 Thessalonians 5:16.

A: "Rejoice evermore"

174. How did God punish Eve for sinning in the Garden of Eden?

A: Greatly increased pain in childbirth (NIV)—Genesis 3:16

175. In the book of Romans, God is quoted as hating what
Bible character?
A: Esau—Romans 9:13

176. Ananias was told to go to a street called _____.
A: Straight—Acts 9:11

177. When Joshua entered the Promised Land, what was
the name of the second city he attacked?
A: Ai—Joshua 7:2-5

178. Who was the first man to suggest that Jonah be thrown
overboard as a result of the storm?
A: Jonah—Jonah 1:12

179. What was the name of the Bible character who because
of his age slept with a beautiful young virgin in order to
keep warm?
A: King David—I Kings 1:1-4

180. Which church in the book of Revelation was called
lukewarm?
A: The church at Laodicea—Revelation 3:14-16

181. When the Israelites complained about eating only
manna, what did God do?
A: He sent quail to them—Numbers 11:31

182. Who was the prophet Samuel speaking to when he
said, "To obey is better than sacrifice"?
A: Saul—1 Samuel 15:20,22

183. In the book of Acts, how many men were chosen to
wait on tables?
A: Seven—Acts 6:2,3

184. What is the name of the man who wanted to buy the
ability to do miracles like Peter and John?
A: Simon—Acts 8:18,19

185. Who were the first twins mentioned in the Bible?
    A: Jacob and Esau—Genesis 25:24-26

186. Quote Philippians 4:13.
    A: "I can do all things through Christ which strength-
    eneth me."

187. What was the name of Adam's son who replaced Abel?
    A: Seth—Genesis 4:25

188. How did the prophet Elijah travel to heaven?
    A: In a whirlwind—2 Kings 2:11

189. Which two New Testament books instruct husbands to
    love their wives?
    A: Ephesians and Colossians—Ephesians 5:25; Co-
    lossians 3:19

190. After Dinah was raped by Shechem, what did her
    brothers do?
    A: Killed all the men of the city—Genesis 34:25

191. In what book of the Bible do we find the words,
    "Though your sins are like scarlet, they shall be as
    white as snow" (NIV)?
    A: Isaiah—Isaiah 1:18

192. King Herod was eaten by _____.
    A: Worms—Acts 12:23

193. In the Old Testament, murderers could flee to what
    cities in order to be safe?
    A: The cities of refuge—Numbers 35:6

194. Which disciple objected to Mary washing Jesus' feet
    with perfume?
    A: Judas—John 12:3-5

195. What is the eighth book of the Bible?
    A: Ruth

196. To whom was Paul speaking when he said, "Let no man despise thy youth"?
     A: Timothy—1 Timothy 4:12

197. What is the name of the Pharisee who defended the apostles before the Sanhedrin in the book of Acts?
     A: Gamaliel—Acts 5:34-39

198. Who were the first Gentiles in Caesarea to be converted to Christianity?
     A: Cornelius and his family—Acts 10:30-48

199. What is the name of the queen for whom the Ethiopian eunuch worked?
     A: Candace—Acts 8:27

200. Which is the longest book in the New Testament?
     a. Matthew   b. Luke   c. Romans
     d. Revelation
     A: "B" or Luke

201. What is the name of the Bible character who said, "Let me inherit a double portion of your spirit" (NIV)?
     A: Elisha—2 Kings 2:9

202. When Philip met the Ethiopian eunuch, he was reading from the book of which prophet?
     A: Isaiah (NIV); Esaias (KJV)—Acts 8:26-28

203. Quote 1 Thessalonians 5:18.
     A: "In everything give thanks: for this is the will of God in Christ Jesus concerning you"

204. In the book of Philemon, what is the name of the servant for whom Paul was making an appeal?
     A: Onesimus—Philemon 10

205. What were the names of Job's three friends?
     A: Eliphas, Bildad, Zophar—Job 2:11

206. As a result of Adam's sin, what became cursed?

A: The ground—Genesis 3:17

207. Who does James suggest will be judged more strictly than others?

A: Teachers (NIV); masters (KJV)—James 3:1

208. What is the name of the man whom King David made drunk?

A: Uriah—2 Samuel 11:12,13

209. The book of Romans has how many chapters?

A: Sixteen

210. Lydia, the seller of purple, was from which city?

A: Thyatira—Acts 16:14

211. In what book of the Bible did Paul state that people who do not work should not eat?

A: 2 Thessalonians—2 Thessalonians 3:10

212. What New Testament book tells the story of a man eating a book (or scroll)?

A: Revelation—Revelation 10:9,10

213. In what book of the Bible does it talk about Satan accusing believers before God day and night?

A: Revelation—Revelation 12:10

214. In the book of Acts, what was the name of the man who predicted that a famine would spread over the entire Roman world?

A: Agabus—Acts 11:28

215. What does Proverbs say is a mocker?

A: Wine—Proverbs 20:1

216. The word Armageddon is used only one time in Scripture. In what book of the Bible is this word found?

A: Revelation—Revelation 16:16

217. In what book in the Bible does it suggest that we not eat too much honey?

A: Proverbs—Proverbs 25:16

218. In the book of Colossians there was a man named Justus. What was his famous other name?

A: Jesus—Colossians 4:11

219. Who was the first person mentioned in the Bible as laughing?

A: Sarah—Genesis 18:12,13

220. What does the Bible say was put in charge to bring up to Christ before faith came?

A: The law—Galatians 3:23,24

221. When David had to face Goliath, he picked up:
   a. Three rough stones   b. Five smooth stones
   c. Five rough stones   d. Three smooth stones

A: "B" or five smooth stones—1 Samuel 17:40

222. Which one of Noah's sons looked on Noah's nakedness?

A: Ham—Genesis 9:22

223. What is the name of the priest that Abram met in the valley of Shaveh?

A: Melchizedek—Genesis 14:17,18

224. What is the name of the land that God told Abram to leave?

A: Ur of the Chaldeans—Genesis 15:7

225. In 1 Corinthians, what is the last enemy to be destroyed?

A: Death—1 Corinthians 15:26

226. Which of these did Jesus cure first?
   a. Blindness   b. Leprosy   c. Lameness

A: "B" or leprosy—Matthew 8:2,3

227. What was the name of the man who made a metal snake and put it on a pole?

    A: Moses—Numbers 21:9

228. In what book of the Bible do you find the words, "Remember your Creator in the days of your youth" (NIV)?

    A: Ecclesiastes—Ecclesiastes 12:1

229. Quote Romans 8:28.

    A: "We know that all things work together for good to them that love God, to them who are called according to his purpose"

230. The book of Proverbs suggests that a good medicine is a _____.

    A: Cheerful heart (NIV); merry heart (KJV)—Proverbs 17:22

231. When blind Bartimaeus came to Jesus, he threw something away. What was it?

    A: His cloak—Mark 10:49,50

232. An Israelite man was exempt from war for how long after he was married?

    A: One year—Deuteronomy 24:5

233. King Herod killed all the baby boys in Bethlehem who were _____ years old and under.

    A: Two—Matthew 2:16

234. What was the name of an angel that fought with the dragon in the book of Revelation?

    A: Michael—Revelation 12:7

235. What was the name of Solomon's mother?

    A: Bathsheba—2 Samuel 12:24

236. What did the angels do to the homosexual men of Sodom to protect Lot?

    A: They struck them with blindness—Genesis 19:9-11

237. Why did Adam name his wife Eve?

   A: Because she was the mother of all the living—Genesis 3:20

238. Who said, "I am slow of speech, and of a slow tongue"?

   A: Moses—Exodus 4:10

239. What two things did God say would happen to Eve for disobedience in the Garden of Eden?

   A: Greatly increased pain in childbearing, her husband would rule over her (NIV); multiplied sorrow in childbirth, her husband would rule over her (KJV)—Genesis 3:16

240. Who said there is "a time to weep and a time to laugh"?

   A: Solomon—Ecclesiastes 3:4

241. In the book of Revelation, who held the key to the Abyss (bottomless pit)?

   A: An angel—Revelation 20:1

242. Who said, "How beautiful are the feet of them that preach the gospel of peace"?

   A: Isaiah—Isaiah 52:7; Paul—Romans 10:15

243. Who wore golden bells on the hem of a blue robe?

   A: Aaron—Exodus 28:31-35

244. What was the name of the Bible character who had red hair like a garment all over his body?

   A: Esau—Genesis 25:25

245. When Apollos came from Alexandria, he first preached in what city?

   A: Ephesus—Acts 18:24-26

246. In what New Testament book do you find the words, "What therefore God hath joined together let not man put asunder"?

   A: Mark—Mark 10:9

247. Philip had four daughters who had a special spiritual gift. What was that gift?

A: Prophecy—Acts 21:8,9

248. What is the name of the only man mentioned in the Bible as being bald-headed?

A: Elisha—2 Kings 2:22,23

249. When the angel in the book of Revelation came to bind Satan, what two objects did he have in his hand?

A: Key and chain—Revelation 20:1,2

250. Jesus calls Himself the morning star in what book of the Bible?

A: Revelation—Revelation 22:16

251. What Bible character describes his girlfriend's hair as a flock of goats descending from Gilead?

A: Solomon—Song of Solomon 6:5

252. After Jesus' trial, what color of robe was put on Him?

A: Purple—Mark 15:15-17

253. Which book of the Bible says, "I would rather be a doorkeeper in the house of my God than dwell in the tents of the wicked" (NIV)?

A: Psalms—Psalm 84:10

254. What is the thirtieth book of the Bible?

A: Amos

255. Quote Philippians 4:19.

A: "But my God shall supply all your needs according to his riches in glory by Christ Jesus"

ANSWERS TO FAIRLY DIFFICULT TRIVIA QUESTIONS

1. Name the man who kept some of the spoils after the battle of Jericho and brought punishment to Israel.
   A: Achan—Joshua 7:1

2. How many of Jesus' brothers wrote books of the Bible?
   A: Two, James and Jude—Matthew 13:55

3. What was the name of Hosea's wife?
   A: Gomer—Hosea 1:3

4. What woman in the Bible tried to seduce a handsome slave?
   A: Potiphar's wife—Genesis 39:1,7

5. What was the name of the king who made a speech and as a result was eaten by worms?
   A: Herod (Agrippa the First)—Acts 12:21-23

6. Miriam and Aaron were upset with Moses because he married a woman who was an _____
   A: Ethiopian—Numbers 12:1

7. How many of the clean animals did Noah take into the Ark?
   A: Seven pairs of clean and one pair of unclean—Genesis 7:2

8. What was the name of a Bible character who told a riddle about a lion?
   A: Samson—Judges 14:12-14

9. There was a very rich man who was a disciple of Jesus What was his name?

   A: Joseph of Arimathea—Matthew 27:57

10. What was the name of the queen who was thrown out of a window?

    A: Jezebel—2 King 9:30-33

11. Solomon said that something "biteth like a serpent, stingeth like an adder." What was it?

    A: Wine—Proverbs 23:31,32

12. What was the name of the city where King Ahasuerus lived?

    A: Shushan—Esther 1:2

13. David is to a sling as Samson is to _____

    A: The jawbone of an ass—1 Samuel 17:40; Judges 15:16

14. How many times did Noah send the dove from the Ark?

    A: Three—Genesis 8:8-12

15. Who had shoes that lasted for forty years and did not wear out?

    A: The children of Israel in the wilderness—Deuteronomy 29:5

16. What is the name of the father who had two daughters married to the same man?

    A: Laban—Genesis 29:16-28

17. How many years were the Israelites in bondage as slaves?

    A: 400 years—Genesis 15:13

18. King Solomon had how many wives?

    A: 700 wives—1 Kings 11:1,3 (Maybe he wasn't so wise after all!)

19. Name the two men who entertained angels unaware.
    A: Abraham and Lot—Genesis 18:1-22, 19:1-22

20. What was the name of the prophet who was swept away
    by a whirlwind?
    A: Elijah—2 Kings 2:11

21. The Sabeans took his oxen and his donkeys, the light-
    ning killed his sheep, the Chaldeans stole his camels,
    and his servants were killed. To whom did all these
    things happen?
    A: Job—Job 1:14-19

22. Who dreamed about a ladder which reached up to
    heaven?
    A: Jacob—Genesis 28:10-12

23. To whom were the following words addressed? "Get
    thee out of thy country, and from thy kindred, and from
    thy father's house, unto a land that I will shew thee."
    A: Abram—Genesis 12:1

24. What Bible character was called "The Gloomy Prophet"?
    A: Jeremiah—Jeremiah 25:11

25. The man called Gehazi was a:
    a. Prophet   b. Servant   c. King
    d. Lawyer   e. Wicked priest
    A: "B" or servant—2 Kings 4:12

26. What is the name of the first of the twelve disciples to be
    murdered?
    A: James—Acts 12:1,2

27. David the shepherd was how old when he became King
    of Israel?
    A: Thirty years old—2 Samuel 5:4

28. Who owned dishes that were pure gold?
    A: King Solomon—1 Kings 10:21

29. Someone came to Pilate and begged for the body of the crucified Jesus. Who was he?

A: Joseph of Arimathea—Matthew 27:57,58

30. In what book of the Bible do you find the following words? "For God shall bring every work into judgment, with every secret thing, whether it be good, or whether it be evil."

A: Ecclesiastes—Ecclesiastes 12:14

31. What was Lot's relationship with Abraham?

A: His nephew—Genesis 12:5

32. What is the name of the town that is called "City of Palm Trees"?

A: Jericho—Deuteronomy 34:3

33. Shem is to Noah as David is to _____.

A: Jesse (son to father)—Genesis 5:32; Acts 13:22

34. What was Jacob's relationship to Laban?

A: Nephew and son-in-law—Genesis 28:1,2; 29:16-28

35. What is the name of the first New Testament martyr?

A: John the Baptist—Matthew 14:10

36. Name the pool that had five porches.

A: The pool at Bethesda—John 5:2

37. Which came first—the Tower of Babel or the Flood?

A: The Flood—Genesis 7-9, Genesis 11

38. Lazarus is to Jesus as Eutychus is to _____

A: Paul (he raised from the dead to he who healed)— John 11:43-45; Acts 20:7-12

39. There was a silversmith in Ephesus by the name of _____.

A: Demetrius—Acts 19:24

40. What is the name of the Bible character that preached in a valley full of dead men's bones?

    A: Ezekiel—Ezekiel 37:1-14

41. How old was Joseph when Pharaoh made him a ruler?

    A: Thirty years old—Genesis 41:46

42. Apollos was a:

    a. King   b. God   c. Learned Jew
    d. Maker of tents

    A: "C" or a learned Jew—Acts 18:24

43. What was the name of the man who helped an African to understand the Scriptures?

    A: Philip—Acts 8:26-35

44. What Bible character used salt to purify drinking water?

    A: Elisha—2 Kings 2:20-22

45. How old was Moses when he died?

    A: 120 years old—Deuteronomy 34:7

46. Something very special happened to a certain man when he was 600 years old. Who was he and what happened?

    A: Noah, and it began to rain—Genesis 7:11

47. How many times did the boy who Elisha raised from the dead sneeze?

    A: Seven times—2 Kings 4:32-35

48. The Ark that Noah built was thirty cubits high, fifty cubits wide, and _____ cubits long.

    A: 300 cubits long—Genesis 6:15

49. Who said, "This day is this scripture fulfilled in your ears"?

    A: Jesus—Luke 4:14,21

50. What Bible character ate a poor widow's last meal?

    A: Elijah—1 Kings 17:10-15

51. In what book of the Bible does it describe hailstones weighing a talent each (about 100 pounds)?
A: Revelation—Revelation 16:21

52. How many years did it take to build the temple in Jesus' time?
A: Forty-six years—John 2:20

53. Who was the man who ordered a cup to be put into a sack of corn?
A: Joseph—Genesis 44:2

54. There are two orders of angels. Can you name them?
A: Cherubim—Genesis 3:24; Seraphim—Isaiah 6:2

55. Some angels came to speak with Lot. How many angels were there?
A: Two—Genesis 19:1

56. How many psalms are there in the Old Testament?
A: 150 psalms

57. What is the name of the Bible character whose handkerchiefs were used to heal people?
A: Paul—Acts 9:11,12

58. Joab was a:
    a. Scribe   b. Priest   c. King
    d. Soldier   e. Servant
    A: "D" or soldier—2 Samuel 2:24-28

59. What is the name of the man who was called "The Supplanter"?
A: Jacob—Genesis 27:36

60. What relationship was Mordecai to Esther?
A: Cousin—Esther 2:5-7

61. What is the name of the boy who was sent out into the desert to die with his mother?
A: Ishmael—Genesis 16:15; 21:14

62. What is the name of the man who offered thirty changes of garments for solving a riddle?
A: Samson—Judges 14:12-18

63. What was the name of a leper who was also the captain of the host of the King of Syria?
A: Naaman—2 Kings 5:1

64. Who asked for the head of John the Baptist and got it?
A: The daughter of Herodias—Matthew 14:6-11

65. What are the three most famous heads of hair mentioned in the Bible?
A: Samson—Judges 16:17; Absalom—2 Samuel 14:25, 26; the woman who wiped the tears from Jesus' feet with her hair—Luke 7:44

66. What was the name of the Egyptian who bought Joseph from the Midianites?
A: Potiphar—Genesis 37:28,36

67. One of Joseph's brothers said, "Let us not kill him." Who was that brother?
A: Reuben—Genesis 37:21-23

68. Who could be called the great hunter of the Bible? (He also loved red meat.)
A: Esau—Genesis 25:25-28

69. The Gibeonites would have been killed by Joshua if it had not been for their old clothes, old shoes, and what kind of bread?
A: Dry and moldy bread—Joshua 9:3-5,12

70. When Joseph's brothers first came to Egypt, he put them into jail for:
a. 1 day   b. 2 days   c. 3 days   d. 4 days
e. 5 days   f. 6 days
A: "C" or three days—Genesis 42:6,17

71. How many Herods are there in the Bible?

    A: Three: Herod the Great—Matthew 2:1-20; Herod Antipas—Matthew 14:1-11; Mark 6:16-28; Luke 3:1-19; 9:7-9; 13:31; 23:7-15; Acts 4:27; Herod Agrippa the First—Acts 12:1-23

72. What type of wood did Noah use when he built the Ark?

    A: Gopher wood—Genesis 6:14

73. How many elders did Moses appoint to help him share the load of dealing with the children of Israel?

    A: Seventy—Numbers 11:16,17

74. Who wrote the book of Lamentations?

    A: Jeremiah

75. What three young men had a father who was 500 years old?

    A: Ham, Shem, and Japeth: the sons of Noah—Genesis 5:32

76. There was a certain group of men who could not wear garments that would cause them to sweat. Who were these men?

    A: The priests of Israel—Ezekiel 44:15-18

77. Abraham asked God to spare the city of Sodom if a certain number of righteous people lived there. What was the final figure that God said he would spare the city for?

    A: Ten righteous people—Genesis 18:32

78. In whose tomb was Jesus buried?

    A: Joseph of Arimathea—Matthew 27:57-60

79. What was the name of the woman who cast her young son in the bushes to die?

    A: Hagar—Genesis 21:14,15

80. What was the name of the mother who hid her son in the bulrushes?

    A: Jochebed, the mother of Moses—Exodus 2:3; 6:20

81. Jesus cursed three cities. What were their names?

    A: Chorazin, Bethsaida, and Capernaum—Matthew 11:21-23

82. What was the name of the country in which Jesus healed two demon-possessed individuals?

    A: Gadarenes or Gergesenes—Matthew 8:28

83. How many loaves of bread did Jesus use in feeding the 4000?

    A: Seven—Matthew 15:36-38

84. Abraham left what country?

    A: Ur of the Chaldees—Genesis 11:31

85. When Philip met the Ethiopian eunuch, he was reading from what book in the Old Testament?

    A: Isaiah—Acts 8:27-30

86. Paul preached on Mars' Hill. In what city is Mars' Hill located?

    A: Athens—Acts 17:15,22

87. Into how many parts did the soldiers divide Jesus' garments?

    A: Four parts—John 19:23

88. What was the name of Jacob's firstborn child?

    A: Reuben—Genesis 35:23

89. When Jacob followed Esau out of his mother's womb, he was holding onto what?

    A: Esau's heel—Genesis 25:23-26

90. What happened to Jacob when he wrestled with God?

    A: He became lame—Genesis 32:24-31

91. How many times did the children of Israel march around the city of Jericho?

    a. 2   b. 7   c. 13   d. 21   e. 49

    A: "C" or 13—Joshua 6:1-4

92. What was the name of the wilderness in which John the Baptist preached?

    A: Judea—Matthew 3:1

93. What caused the large fish to vomit Jonah onto dry land?

    A: God spoke to the fish—Jonah 2:10

94. Who cast down his rod before Pharaoh and the rod became a serpent?

    A: Aaron—Exodus 7:10

95. Who said, "The dog is turned to his own vomit again"?

    A: Peter—2 Peter 2:20-22

96. "At midnight _____ and _____ prayed, and sang praises unto God; and the prisoners heard them."

    A: Paul and Silas—Acts 16:25

97. God opened the mouth of a donkey and the donkey spoke to _____.

    A: Balaam—Numbers 22:28

98. What was the name of the centurion from Caesarea who was part of the Italian band?

    A: Cornelius—Acts 10:1

99. What was the name of Aquila's wife?

    A: Priscilla—Acts 18:2

100. What was the name of the man who carried the cross for Jesus?

    A: Simon the Cyrene—Matthew 27:32

101. To whom was the following spoken? "Go near and join thyself to this chariot."

A: Philip—Acts 8:29

102. What was the name of Timothy's mother?

A: Eunice—2 Timothy 1:5

103. Paul the Apostle was born in what city?

A: Tarsus—Acts 9:11

104. What was the name of the prophet who foretold that Jesus would be born in Bethlehem?

A: Micah—Micah 5:2

105. What relationship was Lois to Timothy?

A: His grandmother—2 Timothy 1:5

106. "As it is written, _____ have I loved, but _____ have I hated."

A: Jacob, Esau—Romans 9:13

107. What is the name of the Old Testament prophet who foretold the virgin birth?

A: Isaiah—Isaiah 7:14

108. To whom was the following spoken? "Silver and gold have I none; but such as I have give I thee: In the name of Jesus Christ of Nazareth rise up and walk."

A: Peter was speaking to the lame beggar at the temple—Acts 3:1-6

109. What is the name of the woman who hid two Israelite spies on the roof of her house?

A: Rahab—Joshua 2:1-6

110. What Bible character saw a city coming down out of heaven?

A: John—Revelation 21:2

111. What is the name of the Bible character who went to visit the witch of Endor?

    A: King Saul—1 Samuel 28:7,8

112. A Christian who returns to a life of sin is likened to which animals?

    A: A dog and a sow—2 Peter 2:20-22

113. In what book of the Bible does it talk about blood running so deep that it reaches up to the bridles of horses?

    A: Revelation—Revelation 14:20

114. The furnace into which Shadrach, Meshach, and Abednego were tossed was heated how many times hotter than usual?

    A: Seven—Daniel 3:19

115. How many times did Jacob bow as he approached Esau?

    A: Seven—Genesis 33:1-3

116. What were the names of the two believers who discipled Apollos?

    A: Priscilla and Aquila—Acts 18:24-26

117. What was the name of Mordecai's cousin whom he brought up?

    A: Esther or Hadassah—Esther 2:7

118. What is the name of the tree that stands on both sides of the river of the water of life in the book of Revelation?

    A: The tree of life—Revelation 22:1,2

119. What is the name of the Bible character who got leprosy by sticking his hand inside his cloak?

    A: Moses—Exodus 4:6

120. Jesus said He could call on His Father for how many legions of angels?

A: More than twelve—Matthew 26:53

121. What was the occupation of Jairus?

A: He was a ruler of the synagogue—Luke 8:41

122. In what two books of the Bible do we find the phrase, "Be not weary in well doing"?

A: 2 Thessalonians and Galatians—2 Thessalonians 3:13; Galatians 6:9

123. What was the first command the Bible mentions that God gave to Adam and Eve?

A: Be fruitful and multiply—Genesis 1:28

124. What was the name of the Bible character who was called "mighty in the Scriptures"?

A: Apollos—Acts 18:24

125. The Year of Jubilee comes how often for the Israelites?

A: Every 50 years—Leviticus 25:10,11

126. What will the gates of the holy city be made of?

A: Pearls—Revelation 21:21

127. How many bowls of water did Gideon squeeze out of his fleece?

A: One—Judges 6:38

128. Satan smote Job with _____ from the soles of his feet to the top of his head.

A: Painful sores (NIV); sore boils (KJV)—Job 2:7

129. Who suggested that it is not wise to spend too much time at your neighbor's house?

A: Solomon—Proverbs 25:17

130. What Bible character said, "Almost thou persuadest me to be a Christian"?

A: King Agrippa—Acts 26:27,28

131. David took two things from Saul while he was asleep.
   What were they?
   A: A spear and a waterjug—1 Samuel 26:7,12

132. What is the name of the Bible character who took all of
   the gold articles out of Solomon's temple?
   A: Nebuchadnezzar—2 Kings 24:11,13

133. In what book of the Bible do we read the words, "It is
   required in stewards that a man be found faithful"?
   A: 1 Corinthians—1 Corinthians 4:2

134. Where did Job live?
   a. Puz   b. Buz   c. Uz   d. Luz   e. Zuz
   A: "C" or Uz—Job 1:1

135. What was the name of Elisha's servant?
   A: Gehazi—2 Kings 4:25

136. In what book of the Bible do we find the story about the
   sun standing still?
   A: Joshua—Joshua 10:12-14

137. Which men wanted to kill Lazarus?
   A: The chief priests—John 12:10

138. What color was manna?
   a. Yellowish   b. Reddish   c. Brownish
   d. White
   A: "D" or white—Exodus 16:31

139. What two items that touched Paul were used then to
   heal people?
   A: Handkerchiefs and aprons—Acts 19:11,12

140. In the Promised Land there were _____ cities of
   refuge.
   A: Six—Numbers 35:6

141. Where does the Bible suggest that too much study is hard on the body?
A: Ecclesiastes—Ecclesiastes 12:12

142. Ruth and Boaz had a son named _____.
A: Obed—Ruth 4:13-17

143. In what book of the Bible do we find the words, "He who wins souls is wise" (NIV)?
A: Proverbs—Proverbs 11:30

144. Zacchaeus repaid to the people he had cheated how many times the amount?
A: Four—Luke 19:8

145. Name the New Testament book that was written to Gaius.
A: 3 John

146. In what book of the Bible do we read the words, "For the love of money is the root of all evil"?
A: 1 Timothy—1 Timothy 6:10

147. The poles used in carrying the Ark of the Covenant were made out of what kind of wood?
A: Acacia (NIV); shittim (KJV)—Exodus 25:10-16

148. What was the other name of the Bible character called Didymus?
A: Thomas—John 20:24

149. Who is the judge and defender of widows?
A: God—Psalm 68:5

150. Does the Bible say that husbands should submit to their wives?
A: Yes—Ephesians 5:21

151. Who said that the Jews had holes in their purses?
A: God, through the prophet Haggai—Haggai 1:6

152. Who is likened to a gold ring in a pig's snout?

    A: A beautiful woman lacking discretion—Proverbs 11:22

153. At what time of day did Eutychus go to sleep and fall out of the window?

    A: Midnight—Acts 20:7-9

154. In what book of the Bible do you find the words, "It is more blessed to give than to receive"?

    A: Acts—Acts 20:35

155. What two men were candidates for the position of the twelfth apostle after Judas' death?

    A: Joseph (called Barsabbas) and Matthias—Acts 1:23

156. What is the name of the man who replaced Judas as the twelfth apostle?

    A: Matthias—Acts 1:26

157. Earthly treasures are destroyed by three things. What are they?

    A: Moths, rust, and thieves—Matthew 6:19

158. In what book of the Bible do you find the words, "Man looks at the outward appearance, but the Lord looks at the heart" (NIV)?

    A: 1 Samuel—1 Samuel 16:7

159. According to Proverbs, the tongue of the wise brings what?

    A: Healing (NIV); health (KJV)—Proverbs 12:18

160. At what time of day is it not good to loudly bless your neighbor?

    A: Early in the morning—Proverbs 27:14

161. How many horns did the goat in Daniel's second vision have?

    A: One—Daniel 8:5

162. What was the name of Moses' father?
A: Amram—Exodus 6:20

163. Who said, "But godliness with contentment is great gain"?
A: Paul—1 Timothy 6:6

164. In what book of the Bible are we told to cast our bread upon the waters?
A: Ecclesiastes—Ecclesiastes 11:1

165. What was the name of the boy who was left under a bush to die?
A: Ishmael—Genesis 16:16; 21:14-16

166. In order to be on the church widow's list, how old did a widow need to be?
A: Sixty years old—1 Timothy 5:9

167. What was on each of the four corners of the bronze altar in the tabernacle?
A: A horn—Exodus 27:2

168. The book of 1 Chronicles spends most of its pages discussing which Bible character?
A: David

169. King Og's bed was made of what kind of metal?
a. Gold   b. Iron   c. Silver   d. Steel
e. Brass
A: "B" or iron—Deuteronomy 3:11

170. Paul asked Timothy to bring him two items while he was in prison. What were those items?
A: Cloak and scrolls (books—KJV)—2 Timothy 4:13

171. What woman in the Bible faked a rape because she was mad?
A: Potiphar's wife—Genesis 39:10-15

172. What was Tabitha's other name?
    A: Dorcas—Acts 9:36

173. What did Jesus and His disciples cross just before He was arrested?
    A: The Kidron Valley (NIV); the brook Cedron (KJV)—John 18:1-3

174. What does the Bible say cannot be bought for any price?
    A: Love—Song of Solomon 8:7

175. The Bible says that male babies should be circumcised when they are how old?
    A: Eight days—Leviticus 12:3

176. What is the name of the servant girl who answered the door when Peter escaped from prison?
    A: Rhoda—Acts 12:13

177. In the story of the rich man and Lazarus, how many brothers did the rich man have?
    A: Five—Luke 16:27,28

178. How old was Isaac when he married Rebekah?
    A: Forty—Genesis 25:20

179. When the kings of the East march westward, what river will dry up?
    A: Euphrates—Revelation 16:12

180. What does "manna" mean?
    A: "What is it?"—Exodus 16:15

181. What are the names of the two women who fought over who would eat mandrakes?
    A: Leah and Rachel—Genesis 30:14-16

182. Where was the only place a Nazarite could cut his hair?
    A: At the entrance to the Tent of Meeting (NIV); at the door of the tabernacle (KJV)—Numbers 6:18

183. The book of Proverbs names four things that are stately in their stride. What are they?

    A: A lion, a rooster (greyhound—KJV), a he-goat, a king—Proverbs 30:29-31

184. In the book of Acts, Peter had a vision that repeated itself how many times?

    A: Three—Acts 10:9-16

185. In the book of Revelation, what spice did the merchants of the earth sell to Babylon?

    A: Cinnamon—Revelation 18:11-13

186. Paul the apostle was stoned in what city?

    A: Lystra—Acts 14:8-19

187. What is the name of the man who was ready to kill his son because he ate honey?

    A: Saul—1 Samuel 14:43,44

188. What is the name of the man who was to provide for the needs of Mephibosheth?

    A: Ziba—2 Samuel 9:9,10

189. Manoah had a famous son. What was his name?

    A: Samson—Judges 13:2,3,24

190. When Abimelech set fire to the tower of Shechem, how many people died in the flames?

    A: About 1000—Judges 9:47-49

191. Who does the Bible say goes around and whispers, peeps, and mutters?

    A: Mediums and spiritists (NIV); wizards (KJV)—Isaiah 8:19,20

192. In what book of the Bible do we find mention of a mother eagle stirring up her nest?

    A: Deuteronomy—Deuteronomy 32:11

193. Who was the first person mentioned in the Bible as being put into prison?
A: Joseph—Genesis 39:20

194. In which book of the Bible do we find mention of a synagogue of Satan?
A: Revelation—Revelation 2:9

195. In the Old Testament, what particular people could not "make baldness upon their head" or cut off the edges of their beards?
A: Priests—Leviticus 21:5

196. Who said that we should not curse rich people from our bedroom?
A: Solomon—Ecclesiastes 10:20

197. How many times is the phrase "born again" mentioned in the Bible?
A: Two—John 3:3,7

198. How many times does the word trinity appear in the Bible?
A: None

199. What Bible character fell on his face and laughed?
A: Abraham—Genesis 17:17

200. What Bible character said that laughter is mad (or foolish—NIV)?
A: Solomon—Ecclesiastes 2:2

201. Who said that even in laughter the heart is sorrowful (aches)?
A: Solomon—Proverbs 14:13

202. In what book of the Bible does it say that, "A feast is made for laughter"?
A: Ecclesiastes—Ecclesiastes 10:19

203. What Bible character said, "Let your laughter be turned to mourning"?

A: James—James 4:9

204. What Bible character said, "The fear of the Lord, that is wisdom; and to depart from evil is understanding"?

A: Job—Job 28:28

205. What caused the flood waters to recede from the face of the earth?

A: A wind—Genesis 8:1

206. How many years did Noah live after the flood?

A: Three hundred fifty—Genesis 9:28

207. What kind of grain did Boaz give to Ruth?

A: Barley—Ruth 3:15

208. In the book of Exodus, what was the color of the priest's robe?

A: Blue—Exodus 28:31

209. Saul was hiding in the _____ when he was to be presented as the king of Israel.

A: Baggage (NIV)—1 Samuel 10:21-24

210. What was the name of Aaron's wife?

A: Elisheba—Exodus 6:23

211. Jesus was a high priest after the order of _____.

A: Melchizedek—Hebrews 5:5,6

212. Paul and Silas prayed at what time of day while they were in jail?

A: Midnight—Acts 16:25

213. In what book of the Bible do you find the statement, "Thy navel is like a round goblet"?

A: Song of Solomon (Song of Songs—NIV)—Song of Solomon 7:2

214. Who were called, "Liars, evil beasts, slow bellies"?
A: The Cretans—Titus 1:12

215. In the book of Luke, who took away the key of knowledge?
A: The lawyers—Luke 11:52

216. In what book of the Bible do we find the first mention of a holy kiss?
A: Romans—Romans 16:16

217. Who sneezed seven times in the Bible?
A: The Shunammite's son—2 Kings 4:35,36

218. In which book of the Bible do we find the country of Spain mentioned?
A: Romans—Romans 15:24,28

219. In what book of the Bible do we find mention of birthing stools?
A: Exodus—Exodus 1:15-17

220. God said that anyone who would kill Cain would receive from Him _____ vengeance.
a. Threefold   b. Sevenfold   c. Tenfold
A: "B" or sevenfold—Genesis 4:15

221. What were the names of Noah's three daughters-in-law?
A: The Bible does not say

222. What was the sign of the covenant between Abram and God?
A: Circumcision—Genesis 17:9-14

223. Who said, "Is anything too hard for the Lord?" (NIV)
A: God Himself—Genesis 18:13,14

224. What did Lot offer to the men of the city of Sodom so they would not take the two angels?
A: His two daughters—Genesis 19:6-8

225. The division of angels called seraphs (seraphims—KJV) have how many wings?

A: Six—Isaiah 6:2

226. Who was called the king of righteousness in the book of Hebrews?

A: Melchizedek—Hebrews 7:1,2

227. In what book of the Bible does it talk about God giving names to all of the stars?

A: Psalms—Psalm 147:4

228. Name the city in which Paul had his hair cut off because of a vow.

A: Cenchrea—Acts 18:18

229. On the sixth day the children of Israel were to gather how many omers of manna for each person?

A: Two—Exodus 16:22

230. Who had the first navy mentioned in the Bible?

A: King Solomon—1 Kings 9:26,27

231. To whom did Jesus say, "Thou gavest me no kiss"?

A: Simon the Pharisee—Luke 7:44,45

232. In the book of Proverbs, the virtuous woman clothed her entire family in what color?

A: Scarlet—Proverbs 31:21

233. What was the former name for the town of Bethel?

A: Luz—Judges 1:23

234. The eighth plague that the Egyptians experienced was the plague of locusts. A strong wind carried the locusts away in which direction?

A: East into the Red Sea—Exodus 10:19

ANSWERS TO HARD TRIVIA QUESTIONS

1. Who was hung on a gallows fifty cubits (about seventy-five feet) high?
   A: Haman—Esther 7:9,10

2. What were the names of the first and last judges of Israel?
   A: Othniel—Judges 1:13; 3:9; and Samuel—1 Samuel 7:8

3. Who was the individual who watched over Baby Moses while he floated in the bulrushes?
   A: His sister—Exodus 2:4

4. What was the name of the mother who made a little coat for her son every year?
   A: Hannah for Samuel—1 Samuel 1:20; 2:18,19

5. What Bible prophet spoke of the killing of the children?
   A: Jeremiah—Jeremiah 31:15

6. What type of bird did Noah first send forth from the Ark?
   A: A raven—Genesis 8:6,7

7. The name of David's first wife was _____.
   A: Michal—1 Samuel 18:27

8. The title written above Jesus' cross said, "JESUS OF NAZARETH THE KING OF THE JEWS." Name the three languages that the title was written in.
   A: Greek, Latin, and Hebrew—John 19:19,20

9. Because of Achan's sin he was stoned in the valley of
   _____.
   A: Achor—Joshua 7:24-26

10. What was the name of the sorcerer who was struck blind
    by Paul the apostle?
    A: Elymas—Acts 13:6-12

11. After Paul's shipwreck he swam to the island of _____.
    A: Melita—Acts 27:41-44; 28:1

12. What was the name of the wife of both Nabal and King
    David?
    A: Abigail—1 Samuel 25:3,42

13. Which of Joseph's brothers was left behind as a hostage
    when the other nine returned to bring Benjamin to
    Egypt?
    A: Simeon—Genesis 42:18-20,24

14. In order to win the battle with Amalek, Aaron and Hur
    helped Moses by _____.
    A: Holding up his hands—Exodus 17:11-13

15. Zipporah had a very famous husband. What was his
    name?
    A: Moses—Exodus 2:21

16. What was the name of the wife of Lapidoth and what is
    she famous for?
    A: Deborah, and she was the first woman judge of
       Israel—Judges 4:4,5

17. When David scrabbled on the doors of the gate, and let
    spittle fall down on his beard, and pretended to be crazy,
    he was doing so because he was afraid of _____.
    A: Achish, the king of Gath—1 Samuel 21:12-15

18. In what book of the Bible do you find the following
    words: "As a jewel of gold in a swine's snout..."?
    A: Proverbs—Proverbs 11:22

19. What was Nebuchadnezzar's other name?
    A: Belshazzar—Daniel 5:2

20. "The Lord hath made all things for himself: yea, even the wicked for _____."
    A: The day of evil—Proverbs 16:4

21. Hannah was the mother of Samuel. What was the name of Hannah's husband?
    A: Elkanah—1 Samuel 1:8

22. To whom did God tell to go and marry a prostitute?
    A: Hosea—Hosea 1:2

23. What is the name of the Bible character who saw a roll flying in the sky?
    A: Zechariah—Zechariah 5:1

24. Two men in the Bible had the same name. One was a very poor man and the other was a friend of Jesus. What was their common name?
    A: Lazarus—Luke 16:20; John 11; 12:1

25. When Peter was released from prison, he knocked at the door of the gate and a certain person came to answer his knock. Who was that individual?
    A: Rhoda—Acts 12:13

26. People will be thrown into the lake of fire because
    _____.
    A: Their names are not written in the Book of Life—Revelation 20:15

27. When Paul was shipwrecked on the island of Melita, he stayed with the chief man on the island. Who was this man?
    A: Publius—Acts 28:1,7

28. What is the name of the man who slept in the land of Nod?
    A: Cain—Genesis 4:16

29. "And they gave forth their lots; and the lot fell upon
_____; and he was numbered with the eleven apostles."
A: Matthias—Acts 1:26

30. What was the name of the vagabond Jewish exorcists
who tried to cast the evil spirit out of a man? "And the
man in whom the evil spirit was leaped on them, and
overcame them, and prevailed against them, so that
they fled out of that house naked and wounded."
A: The seven sons of Sceva—Acts 19:13-16

31. "And Cush begat _____. He was a mighty hunter
before the Lord."
A: Nimrod—Genesis 10:8,9

32. What was the name of the queen that was replaced by
Esther?
A: Vashti—Esther 1:17

33. What Bible character was called "The Tishbite"?
A: Elijah—1 Kings 17:1

34. Who in the Bible asked God to put his tears in a bottle?
A: David—Psalm 56:8

35. What was the name of the archangel who debated with
the devil?
A: Michael—Jude 9

36. What does the word Ichabod mean?
A: The glory is departed—1 Samuel 4:21

37. The apostle Peter was known by three names. What
were they?
A: Cephas—John 1:42; Simon—Matthew 10:2; Simeon—Acts 15:14

38. What was the name of the runaway slave who went back
to his master?
A: Onesimus—Philemon 10-12

39. Who said, "Am I a dog, that thou comest to me with staves"?

    A: Goliath—1 Samuel 17:43

40. What is the name of the partially blind man who was ninety-eight years old and was very fat who fell off his seat and broke his neck?

    A: Eli—1 Samuel 4:15,18

41. What is the shortest verse in the Bible?

    A: Jesus wept—John 11:35

42. What Bible character accidentally hanged himself in a tree?

    A: Absalom—2 Samuel 18:9,10

43. How many children did Jacob have?

    a. 9   b. 11   c. 13   d. 15   e. 17

    A: "C" or thirteen—Genesis 29,30,35 (twelve sons, one daughter)

44. How many days was Noah on the Ark before it started to rain?

    A: Seven—Genesis 7:1,4

45. What type of bird fed the prophet Elijah?

    A: A raven—1 Kings 17:1,6

46. What is the longest chapter in the Bible?

    A: Psalm 119 with 176 verses

47. In what book of the Bible do you find the following words: "Can the Ethiopian change his skin, or the leopard his spots"?

    A: Jeremiah—Jeremiah 13:23

48. When a certain king put on a feast, God's handwriting appeared on the wall and startled everyone present. What is the name of this king?

    A: Belshazzar—Daniel 5

49. What is the name of the woman who slept at the feet of her future husband?

A: Ruth—Ruth 3:7-9; 4:10

50. What type of food did the brothers of Joseph eat after they threw him into the pit?

A: Bread—Genesis 37:23-25

51. A scarlet cord in a window saved someone and their family. Who was this person?

A: Rahab—Joshua 2:1,18

52. In a contest for good-looking men, four men won because they were vegetarians and God blessed them. Who were these men?

A: Daniel, Hananiah, Mishael, and Azariah—Daniel 1:11-16

53. Elisha cursed forty-two children because they made fun of him and mocked him. What did they say?

A: "Go up, thou bald head; go up, thou bald head"—2 Kings 2:15,23

54. As a result of the curse of Elisha, what happened to the forty-two children?

A: Two she-bears came out of the woods and tore them apart—2 Kings 2:15,23,24

55. When God expelled Adam and Eve from the Garden of Eden, he placed Cherubim at the _____ of the Garden of Eden.

A: East—Genesis 3:24

56. What Bible character drove his chariot furiously?

A: Jehu—2 Kings 9:20

57. What is the name of the left-handed Benjamite who killed King Eglon?

A: Ehud—Judges 3:15-25

58. King Eglon was killed with a dagger that was _____ inches long, and the dagger could not be pulled out because _____.

    A: About eighteen inches long (one cubit), because Eglon was so fat that the fat closed upon the blade so that he could not draw the dagger out of his belly— Judges 3:22

59. What two books in the Bible were written to Theophilus?

    A: Luke and Acts—Luke 1:3; Acts 1:1

60. What Bible character had his lips touched with a live coal?

    A: Isaiah—Isaiah 6:6,7

61. Who was the person who dreamed about a tree which reached to heaven?

    A: Nebuchadnezzar—Daniel 4:4,5,10,11

62. What woman in the Bible had five husbands?

    A: The woman of Samaria (or the woman at the well)— John 4:7,17,18

63. When the magi came to seek Baby Jesus, where did they find Him?

    A: In a house—Matthew 2:1,2,11

64. Who caused bricklayers to go on strike?

    A: Moses—Exodus 1:13,14; 4:29; 5:1; 12:51

65. What Bible character changed dust into lice?

    A: Aaron—Exodus 8:17

66. Who was the man to first organize an orchestra in the Bible?

    A: David—2 Samuel 6:5

67. Of all the books in the Bible, which one does not contain the name of God?

    A: Esther

68. A lost ax head was made to float by _____.
    A: Elisha—2 Kings 6:5-7

69. What person in the Bible walked for forty days without eating?
    A: Elijah—1 Kings 19:2,8

70. Why did Absalom kill his brother Amnon?
    A: Because he raped Tamar—2 Samuel 13:10-32

71. Who paid for the nursing of Moses?
    A: Pharaoh's daughter—Exodus 2:8,9

72. Who committed suicide with his own sword?
    A: Saul—1 Samuel 31:1-5

73. Who committed suicide by hanging himself?
    A: Judas Iscariot—Matthew 27:3-5

74. What king pouted in his bed because he could not buy someone's vineyard?
    A: Ahab—1 Kings 21:2-4

75. King Solomon had another name. What was it?
    A: Jedidiah—2 Samuel 12:24,25

76. Who was the man to build the first city and what was its name?
    A: Cain, and the name of the city was Enoch—Genesis 4:17

77. What woman in the Bible made a pair of kid gloves for her son?
    A: Rebekah—Genesis 27:15,16

78. A certain queen's blood was sprinkled on horses. Who was this queen?
    A: Jezebel—2 Kings 9:30-33

79. Who was the first musician in the Bible? What instruments did he play?

    A: Jubal, and he played the harp and organ—Genesis 4:21

80. What Bible person cut his hair only once a year?

    A: Absalom—2 Samuel 14:25,26

81. Name the gentile king that made Esther his queen.

    A: Ahasuerus—Esther 2:16,17

82. Who said the following and to whom was he speaking? "Because thou hast mocked me: I would there were a sword in mine hand, for now would I kill thee."

    A: Spoken by Balaam to his donkey—Numbers 22:28, 29

83. The mother-in-law of Ruth was Naomi. What was the name of her father-in-law?

    A: Elimelech—Ruth 1:2-4

84. What is the name of the man who was seduced by his daughter-in-law and what was her name?

    A: Judah was seduced by Tamar—Genesis 38:13-18

85. How many times did Balaam hit his donkey before the donkey spoke to him?

    A: Three times—Numbers 22:28

86. How many years were added to Hezekiah's life?

    A: Fifteen—Isaiah 38:5

87. Joash was told to shoot an arrow from the window. What was the arrow called?

    A: The arrow of the Lord's deliverance—2 Kings 13:15-17

88. God gave Hezekiah a sign that he would live longer. What was that sign?

    A: The shadow on the sundial went backward ten degrees—Isaiah 38:8

89. Name the king who had the longest reign in the Bible.
    A: Manasseh (fifty-five years)—2 Chronicles 33:1

90. Which of the prophets was thrown into a dungeon?
    A: Jeremiah—Jeremiah 37:16

91. When a certain king tried to take the place of the priest
    at the altar, he was struck with leprosy. Who was this
    king?
    A: Uzziah—2 Chronicles 26:18-21

92. How was Naaman healed of his leprosy?
    A: He dipped seven times in the Jordan River—2 Kings
       5:1,10,14

93. While _____ was hanging in a tree, he was killed by
    three darts from Joab.
    A: Absalom—2 Samuel 18:14

94. Nicodemus put how many pounds of myrrh and aloes
    on the body of Jesus?
    A: One hundred pounds—John 19:39

95. What was the name of the person who became king
    while he was a little child?
    A: Josiah—2 Kings 22:1

96. Job's friends sat in silence with Job and mourned with
    him for how many days?
    A: Seven days—Job 2:11,13

97. Where was Judas Iscariot buried?
    A: In a potter's field—Matthew 27:3-10

98. Jesus told Nathanael that he had seen him before.
    Where did Jesus see Nathanael?
    A: Under a fig tree—John 1:48

99. In the book of Proverbs, God says he hates how many things?

    A: Seven things (a proud look, a lying tongue, hands that shed innocent blood, a wicked heart, someone willing to be mischievous, a false witness, and someone who sows discord)—Proverbs 6:16

100. The Bible suggests that the average life span is how many years?

    A: Seventy—Psalm 90:10

101. How many barrels of water did Elijah ask the men to pour over the sacrifice on the altar?

    A: twelve—1 Kings 18:33,34

102. Because of offering "strange fire" on the altar of God, how many men died?

    A: Two—Leviticus 10:1,2

103. David disobeyed God and numbered the people. As a result God gave David the choice of one of

    a. 2   b. 3   c. 4   d. 5

    different kinds of punishment.

    A: "B" or three punishments—1 Chronicles 21:10

104. What leader chose his followers by watching how they drank water?

    A: Gideon—Judges 7:5

105. How many stones were placed in the Jordan River after the children of Israel had crossed over on dry land?

    A: Twelve—Joshua 4:3

106. As Joshua and the children of Israel marched around the walls of Jericho, the priests carried trumpets before the Ark of the Lord. How many priests carried trumpets?

    A: Seven—Joshua 6:4

107. When Elijah was on Mt. Carmel, how many times did
     he send his servant to look for a cloud?
     A: Seven—1 Kings 18.42-44

108. The two spies that Rahab hid fled into the mountains
     and hid for how many days?
     A: Three days—Joshua 2:3,22

109. How many men from the tribe of Judah were sent out
     to capture Samson?
     A: Three thousand—Judges 15:11

110. How old was Jehoash when he was crowned king?
     A: Seven years old—2 Kings 11:21

111. This person was brought water from the well at Beth-
     lehem but poured it out on the ground because it
     was brought to him at great risk. Who was this per-
     son?
     A: David—2 Samuel 23:15,16

112. What type of bird was sold for "two for a farthing"?
     A: Sparrow—Matthew 10:29

113. Absalom was riding on a _____ when his hair caught
     in a tree.
     A: Mule—2 Samuel 18:9

114. What did Achan steal from Jericho?
     A: Gold, silver, and a garment—Joshua 7:1,21

115. What Old Testament character wore a "coat of mail"?
     A: Goliath—1 Samuel 17:4,5

116. Name the twelve apostles.
     A: Peter, Andrew, James, John, Philip, Bartholomew
        (Nathaniel), Thomas, Matthew, James, Thaddaeus,
        Simon, Judas Iscariot—Matthew 10:1-4

117. What was the name of the witch that Saul visited?
     A: The witch of Endor—1 Samuel 28:7

118. The word "coffin" is used only once in the entire Bible. Do you know who was buried in this coffin?

A: Joseph—Genesis 50:26

119. The Bible warns men to beware of a woman's eyes. In what book of the Bible do you find this warning?

A: Proverbs—Proverbs 6:25

120. While Joseph was in prison he interpreted dreams for two men. What were the occupations of these two men?

A: Baker and butler—Genesis 40:1-9,16

121. Whose birthday celebration was the first mentioned in the Bible?

A: Pharaoh's—Genesis 40:20

122. In what book of the Bible does it talk about trading a boy for a harlot?

A: Joel—Joel 3:3

123. How many men in the Bible were named Judas?

A: Six—Matthew 10:4; 13:55; Luke 6:16; Acts 5:37; 9:11; 15:22

124. Who received the first kiss that is mentioned in the Bible?

A: Isaac—Genesis 27:26,27

125. "The men of _____ were wicked and sinners before the Lord exceedingly."

A: Sodom—Genesis 13:13

126. In what book of the Bible do we find the first mention of a physician?

A: Jeremiah—Jeremiah 8:22

127. When Jeremiah said that all their heads would be shaved and their beards clipped, who was he speaking about?

A: Moab—Jeremiah 48:36,37

128. Whose lips quivered and bones decayed when he heard the voice of the Lord?

A: Habakkuk—Habakkuk 3:16

129. In what book of the Bible do you find the words, "Thine eyes like the fishpools in Heshbon"?

A: Song of Solomon (Song of Songs—NIV)—Song of Solomon 7:4

130. Who was the first man the Bible says had a dream?

A: Abimelech—Genesis 20:3

131. In what book of the Bible do we find God's punishment of "consumption, and the burning ague"?

A: Leviticus—Leviticus 26:16

132. How many chapters are in the book of Esther?

A: Ten

133. How much money did the innkeeper receive from the Good Samaritan for taking care of the sick man?

A: Two silver coins (NIV); two pence—about 15 cents (KJV)—Luke 10:35

134. In what book of the Bible do we find the first mention of a "lunatic"?

A: Matthew—Matthew 4:24

135. King Solomon had how many horsemen?

A: Twelve thousand—2 Chronicles 9:25

136. In what book of the Bible do we have the first mention of magicians?

A: Genesis—Genesis 41:8

137. Who does the Bible say eats, wipes her mouth, and says, "I've done nothing wrong"?

A: An adulteress—Proverbs 30:20

138. What did David do with Goliath's weapons?

A: He kept them—1 Samuel 17:54

139. In the end of the book of Job, how many camels did
     God give to Job?

     A: Six thousand—Job 42:12

140. When Elijah built the altar on Mount Carmel, how
     many stones did he use?

     A: Twelve—1 Kings 18:31,32

141. What were the names of Pharaoh's two store cities in
     the book of Exodus?

     A: Pithom, Rameses—Exodus 1:11

142. In the book of Ruth, what was Naomi's other name?

     A: Mara—Ruth 1:20

143. In what book of the Bible does God say there will be
     showers of blessing?

     A: Ezekiel—Ezekiel 34:26

144. In which book of the Bible do you read the words, "Be
     sure your sin will find you out"?

     A: Numbers—Numbers 32:23

145. Nabal owned how many goats?

     A: One thousand—1 Samuel 25:2,3

146. When Josiah heard God's law read, he did what?

     A: Tore his robes—2 Chronicles 34:19

147. In what book of the Bible do we find mention of 20,000
     baths of wine and 20,000 baths of oil?

     A: 2 Chronicles—2 Chronicles 2:10

148. In Zechariah's vision of four chariots, what was the
     color of the horses pulling the fourth chariot?

     A: Dappled (NIV); grisled and bay (KJV)—Zechariah
     6:1-3

149. One book in the Bible has the same amount of chapters as there are books in the Bible. What is the name of the book?

    A: Isaiah

150. What was the name of Jonah's father?

    A: Amittai—Jonah 1:1

151. How many chapters are in the book of Nehemiah?

    A: Thirteen

152. What was the occupation of Shiphrah and Puah?

    A: They were Hebrew midwives—Exodus 1:15

153. What animal was never to be cooked in its mother's milk?

    A: A young goat—Exodus 23:19

154. Rahab the harlot hid the two Jewish spies under what?

    A: Flax—Joshua 2:1-6

155. What are the names of the two women who argued over who would get to sleep with their mutual husband?

    A: Leah and Rachel—Genesis 30:14-16

156. Miriam played what kind of musical instrument?

    A: Tambourine (NIV); timbrel (KJV)—Exodus 15:20

157. What does the Bible say manna tasted like?

    A: Wafers with honey—Exodus 16:31; olive oil (NIV)— Numbers 11:8

158. What Bible character was called a wild donkey of a man?

    A: Hagar's son Ishmael (NIV)—Genesis 16:7-12

159. When King Nebuchadnezzar went crazy, his fingernails began to look like _____.

    A: Birds' claws—Daniel 4:33,34

160. What is the last word in the Bible?
    A: Amen—Revelation 22:21

161. What Bible character fell in love with his sister?
    A: Amnon—2 Samuel 13:1,2

162. The prophet Amos tended two things. What were they?
    A: Sheep and sycamore trees—Amos 7:14

163. The Ark of the Testimony or Covenant was covered with what color cloth when it was moved?
    A: Blue—Numbers 4:5,6

164. Who was the first Bible character mentioned as living in a tent?
    A: Jabal—Genesis 4:20

165. What is the name of the Bible character who ran faster than a chariot?
    A: Elijah—1 Kings 18:45,46

166. What three colors were used in sewing the tabernacle curtains?
    A: Blue, purple, and scarlet—Exodus 26:1

167. Who came out with bald heads and raw shoulders after a long siege against the city of Tyre?
    A: Nebuchadnezzar's soldiers—Ezekiel 29:18

168. At what time of day did the sailors going to Rome on the ship with Paul first sense land after the storm?
    A: Midnight—Acts 27:20-27

169. In the book of Acts, how many soldiers guarded Peter while he was in prison?
    A: Sixteen (NIV)—Acts 12:3,4

170. Who was the first man in the Bible mentioned as being sick?
    A: Jacob—Genesis 48:1,2

171. Who was the fourth oldest man in the Bible?

     A: Adam—Genesis 5:5,20,27; 9:29

172. How many yoke of oxen did Job own before tragedy entered his life?

     A: Five hundred—Job 1:3

173. In Elim, the Israelites found 70 palm trees and _____ springs (fountains).

     A: Twelve—Numbers 33:9

174. Moses was told by the Lord to write what on the staff of each leader of the tribes of Israel?

     A: The leader's name—Numbers 17:1,2

175. Hannah was taunted by _____ about not having a baby.

     A: Peninnah—1 Samuel 1:2,4-6

176. Certain Athenian philosophers thought Paul the apostle was a _____.

     A: Babbler—Acts 17:18

177. Zechariah had a vision of a basket (ephah). What was in the basket?

     A: A woman—Zechariah 5:7

178. When King Shishak stole the gold shields from the temple, who replaced them with bronze (brass) shields?

     A: Rehoboam—2 Chronicles 12:9,10

179. In what book of the Bible do we find mention of the name Narcissus?

     A: Romans—Romans 16:11

180. In what book of the Bible do you find the words, "The joy of the Lord is your strength"?

     A: Nehemiah—Nehemiah 8:10

181. Who is the first person in the Bible mentioned as writing a letter?

A: David—2 Samuel 11:14

182. Who received the first letter written in the Bible?

A: Joab—2 Samuel 11:14

183. Who said, "If I perish, I perish"?

A: Esther—Esther 4:15,16

184. Name the shortest book in the Old Testament.

a. Jonah   b. Nehemiah   c. Obadiah
d. Zephaniah   e. Malachi

A: "C" or Obadiah—21 verses

185. The Recabites refused to drink _____.

A: Wine—Jeremiah 35:5,6

186. The woman who poured perfume of Jesus' head carried the perfume in what kind of jar?

A: An alabaster jar (NIV)—Matthew 26:6,7

187. Who does the Bible say was the most humble man?

A: Moses—Numbers 12:3

188. Who was Asenath's famous husband?

A: Joseph—Genesis 41:45

189. Who bored a hole in the lid of a chest so that it could become a bank to hold money?

A: Jehoiada the priest—2 Kings 12:9

190. After feeding the 4000 men, Jesus went where?

A: The vicinity of Magadan (NIV): the coasts of Magdala (KJV)—Matthew 15:38,39

191. What is the name of the prophet who said that Paul would be arrested in Jerusalem?

A: Agabus—Acts 21:10,11

192. When the temple in the Old Testament was moved, what kind of animal skins were put over the Ark of the Testimony or Covenant?

A: Hides of sea cows (NIV); badgers' skins (KJV)— Numbers 4:5,6

193. What was the name of the dying king who was propped up in his chariot for a whole day?

A: Ahab—1 Kings 22:34,35,40

194. The Anakites (Anakims—KJV) and the Emites (Emims— KJV) had a common physical characteristic. What was it?

A: Their tall stature—Deuteronomy 2:10

195. King Solomon had his carriage upholstered in what color of material?

A: Purple—Song of Solomon 3:9,10

196. In which book of the Bible do we find the first mention of the name Satan?

A: 1 Chronicles—1 Chronicles 21:1

197. The invalid had been lying by the pool of Bethesda for how many years?

A: Thirty-eight—John 5:2-5

198. Mary washed Jesus' feet with what kind of perfume?

A: Nard (NIV); spikenard (KJV)—John 12:3

199. What did Jacob name the place where he wrestled with a man?

A: Peniel—Genesis 32:24,30

200. When Jacob wrestled with a man, what were the man's first words to Jacob?

A: "Let me go, for the day breaketh"—Genesis 32:24-26

201. How many men did Esau bring with him when he came to meet Jacob?
    a. 100   b. 200   c. 300   d. 400   e. 500
    A: "D" or four hundred—Genesis 32:6

202. What special physical feature did Leah have?
    A: Her eyes—Genesis 29:17

203. Elisha was plowing the ground with how many yoke of oxen when Elijah found him?
    A: Twelve—1 Kings 19:19

204. In what book of the Bible does it talk about people who could not tell their right hand from their left hand?
    A: Jonah—Jonah 4:11

205. What is the name of the man who raped Dinah?
    A: Shechem—Genesis 34:1,2

206. When Job became ill, his skin turned to what color?
    A: Black—Job 30:30

207. David's delegation to King Hanun had to stay in what town until their beards had grown back?
    A: Jericho—1 Chronicles 19:1-5

208. What woman's name is mentioned most often in the Bible?
    A: Sarah—60 times

209. Gideon was the father of how many sons?
    A: Seventy-one—Judges 8:29-31,35

210. What is the name of the king who had 900 iron chariots?
    A: King Jabin—Judges 4:2,3

211. King Solomon had how many steps to his throne?
    A: Six—1 Kings 10:18-20

212. What was the name of Isaiah's father?
    A: Amoz—Isaiah 1:1

213. David was betrothed to Saul's daughter for how many Philistine foreskins?
    A: One hundred—2 Samuel 3:14

214. After the Philistines cut off Saul's head, they put it in the temple of _____.
    A: Dagon—1 Chronicles 10:8-10

215. Deborah, the Old Testament judge, sat under what kind of tree?
    A: Palm—Judges 4:4,5

216. In the parable of the Good Samaritan, who was the second person to ignore the injured man?
    A: A Levite—Luke 10:30-32

217. When King Ben-Hadad attacked Samaria, how many kings helped him?
    A: Thirty-two—1 Kings 20:1

218. Jonathan, Ishvi, and Malki-Shua had a famous father. What was his name?
    A: Saul—1 Samuel 14:49

219. What is the name of the Bible prophet who was lifted by his hair between heaven and earth to see a vision?
    A: Ezekiel—Ezekiel 8:3

220. What name did Amos call the sinful women of Israel?
    A: Cows of Bashan (NIV)—Amos 4:1

221. Nehemiah went to the keeper of the king's forest to get wood. What was the forest-keeper's name?
    A: Asaph—Nehemiah 2:8

222. When is the first time love is mentioned in the Bible?
    A: When Isaac married Rebekah—Genesis 24:67

223. In which book of the Bible do we find the only mention of the name Lucifer?

    A: Isaiah—Isaiah 14:12

224. What Bible character said, "By my God have I leaped over a wall"?

    A: David—Psalm 18:29

225. Who was the first left-handed man mentioned in the Bible?

    A: Ehud the left-handed Benjamite—Judges 3:15

226. Who called Israel a "backsliding heifer"?

    A: Hosea—Hosea 4:16

227. Who said, "Man is born into trouble, as the sparks fly upward"?

    A: Eliphaz the Temanite—Job 4:1; 5:7

228. The river Pishon flowed out of the Garden of Eden into the land _____, where there was gold.

    A: Havilah—Genesis 2:10,11

229. In what book of the Bible do we find mention of the word stargazers?

    A: Isaiah—Isaiah 47:13

230. The name "Ziz" was _____.

    a. A city   b. A brook   c. A cliff
    d. A soldier   e. A priest   f. None of the
                                              above

    A: "C" or cliff—2 Chronicles 20:16

231. Jazer was _____.

    a. A king   b. A land   c. A priest
    d. A river   e. A servant   f. None of the
                                              above

    A: "B" or a land—Numbers 32:1

232. How old was Adam when he died?
A: Nine hundred and thirty—Genesis 5:5

233. Who was the father of Enoch?
A: Jared—Genesis 5:18

234. How many days after the tops of the mountains appeared did Noah wait before he opened the window of the Ari?
A: Forty—Genesis 8:5,6

235. Who was the famous son of Terah?
A: Abram—Genesis 11:26

236. When Lot left Sodom, what city did he flee to?
A: Zoar—Genesis 19:18-22

237. What are the names of the two children who were born to Lot's two daughters?
A: Moab and Ben-Ammi—Genesis 19:36-38

238. How old was Sarah when she died?

a. 103   b. 112   c. 127   d. 133
A: "C" or 127—Genesis 23:1

239. What were the names of the two wives of Esau who caused Isaac and Rebekah much grief?
A: Judith and Basemath—Genesis 26:34,35

240. Who was the second oldest man in the Bible?
A: Jared—Genesis 5:20,27

241. How old was Enoch when God took him to heaven?
A: Three hundred and sixty-five—Genesis 5:23,24

242. The Israelites hung their harps on what kind of trees?
A: Poplars (NIV); willows (KJV)—Psalm 137:2

243. After baptizing the eunuch, Philip was taken by the Spirit of the Lord to what city?
A: Azotus—Acts 8:38-40

244. How long did Job live after the Lord made him prosperous again?
 A: One hundred and forty years—Job 42:16

245. What was the name of Eli's grandson?
 A: Ichabod—1 Samuel 4:16-21

ANSWERS TO TRIVIA QUESTIONS FOR THE EXPERT

1. What Bible personality was called a half-baked pancake?
   A: Ephraim ("Ephraim is a cake not turned")—Hosea 7:8

2. What was the name of the king who put Jeremiah into a dungeon in which he sank in the mire?
   A: Zedekiah—Jeremiah 38:5,6

3. Absalom caught his hair in what kind of a tree?
   A: Oak—2 Samuel 18:9

4. Four rivers flowed out of the Garden of Eden. What are the names of these four rivers?
   A: Pison, Gihon, Hiddekel, and Euphrates—Genesis 2:10,14

5. Eldad and Medad are famous because of:
   a. Their victory in battle   b. Their prophecy
   c. Their rebellion against Moses
   d. Not in the Bible
   A: "B" or their prophecy—Numbers 11:26-29

6. Muppim, Huppim, and Ard were:
   a. Amramite gods
   b. The words of a chant of the priest of Baal
   c. Three men who rebelled
   d. The sons of Benjamin
   e. Not in the Bible
   A: "D" or sons of Benjamin—Genesis 46:21

7. What was the name of the man who had his head cut off
   and thrown over a wall to Joab?

   A: Sheba—2 Samuel 20:14-22

8. What tribe had 700 left-handed men who could sling
   stones at a hair breadth and not miss?

   A: The Benjamites—Judges 20:15,16

9. What was the name of the secretary of Paul the apostle
   who wrote the book of Romans for Paul?

   A: Tertius—Romans 16:22

10. At Belshazzar's feast a hand wrote on the wall, *"Mene,
    Mene, Tekel, U-pharsin."* What was the interpretation of
    the words?

    A: Mene—God hath numbered thy kingdom, and fin-
    ished it; Tekel—Thou art weighed in the balances,
    and art found wanting; U-pharsin—Thy kingdom is
    divided, and given to the Medes and Persians—
    Daniel 5:25-28

11. What were the weather forecasts Jesus told the Phar-
    isees and Sadducees?

    A: Evening sky red—fair weather; morning sky red—
    stormy weather—Matthew 16:1-3

12. Who was the person called Candace?

    A: Queen of the Ethiopians—Acts 8:27

13. When the seventh seal was opened in the book of
    Revelation, there was silence in heaven for:

    a. A minute   b. A half-hour   c. An hour
    d. A day   e. A month   f. A half-year
    g. A year

    A: "B" or a half-hour—Revelation 8:1

14. In His ministry, Jesus mentioned a region of ten cities.
    What was that region called?

    A: Decapolis—Matthew 4:25

15. What was the name of Blind Bartimaeus's father?
    A: Timaeus—Mark 10:46

16. In what book of the Bible does God tell a certain man not to cover his mustache?
    A: Ezekiel—Ezekiel 24:17

17. When Aaron's rod blossomed, what type of nuts did it yield?
    A: Almonds—Numbers 17:8

18. On the priestly garments a certain fruit was used as a design. What kind of fruit was it?
    A: Pomegranates—Exodus 28:2,34

19. The Old Testament character Job lived in the land of
    _____.
    A: Uz—Job 1:1

20. Who had faces like lions and could run as fast as the gazelles?
    A: The Gadites, part of David's mighty men—1 Chronicles 12:8

21. What does the word Ebenezer mean?
    A: The Lord helped us—1 Samuel 7:12

22. Who fell asleep during a sermon and died as a result?
    A: Eutychus—Acts 20:9

23. When the Ark of the Covenant was being brought back to Jerusalem, the oxen shook the cart and the Ark started to turn over. One man put his hand on the Ark to keep if from falling and died as a result of touching the Ark. Who was this man?
    A: Uzzah—2 Samuel 6:6,7

24. What is the shortest verse in the Old Testament?
    A: Eber, Peleg, Reu—1 Chronicles 1:25

25. Who were the people called the Zamzummims?
    A: A race of giants—Deuteronomy 2:20

26. The first archer mentioned in the Bible was _____.
    A: Ishmael—Genesis 16:16; 21:14,20

27. There are four different colored horses mentioned in the book of Revelation. What were the four different colors?
    A: White, red, black, pale—Revelation 6:1-8

28. What Bible character called himself "a dead dog"?
    A: Mephibosheth—2 Samuel 9:6,8

29. What evangelist had four daughters who prophesied?
    A: Philip—Acts 21:8,9

30. What is the longest word in the Bible?
    A: Mahershalalhashbaz—Isaiah 8:1,3

31. What king slept in a bed that was four cubits (six feet) wide and nine cubits (thirteen feet) long?
    A: Og, the king of Bashan, who was a giant—Deuteronomy 3:11

32. In the book of Revelation a star called _____ fell when the third angel sounded his trumpet.
    A: Wormwood—Revelation 8:10,11

33. What little-boy king had to be hidden in a bedroom for six years to escape the wrath of his wicked grandmother?
    A: Joash—2 Kings 11:1,2

34. The giant Goliath lived in what city?
    A: Gath—1 Samuel 17:4

35. How many proverbs is King Solomon credited in knowing?
    A: Three thousand—1 Kings 4:30,32

36. Who washed his steps with butter?
    A: Job—Job 29:1,6

37. Jeremiah had a secretary. What was his name?
    A: Baruch—Jeremiah 36:10,17,18

38. Who in the Bible is considered the father of all musicians?
    A: Jubal—Genesis 4:21

39. What is the name of the dressmaker who was raised from the dead?
    A: Dorcas—Acts 9:36-40

40. What Bible character's hair stood up on end when he saw a ghost?
    A: Eliphaz ("Then a spirit passed before my face; the hair of my flesh stood up")—Job 4:1,15,16

41. Naomi had two daughters-in-law. One daughter-in-law, Ruth, went with Naomi and the other daughter-in-law, named _____, stayed in the country of Moab.
    A: Orpha—Ruth 1:4,14

42. When Joshua destroyed Jericho he destroyed everyone in the city except for how many households?
    A: One—Joshua 6:17

43. In what book of the Bible do you find a verse that contains every letter except the letter "J"?
    A: Ezra—Ezra 7:21

44. Most young men smile when they kiss a girl, but what Bible character wept when he kissed his sweetheart?
    A: Jacob ("And Jacob kissed Rachel, and lifted up his voice and wept")—Genesis 29:11,18

45. What man in the Bible killed sixty-nine (threescore and nine) of his brothers?
    A: Abimelech, son of Gideon—Judges 9:4,5

46. How much money did the brothers of Joseph make when they sold Joseph into slavery?
    A: Twenty pieces of silver—Genesis 37:28

47. What Bible-song composer is given credit for writing 1005 songs?

A: Solomon—1 Kings 4:30,32

48. Who were Jannes and Jambres?

a. Two of the spies to the Promised Land
b. Two priests in Israel
c. Two men who started a rebellion against Joshua
d. Two of Pharaoh's magicians
e. Two of the children of Reuben

A: "D" or two of Pharaoh's magicians—2 Timothy 3:8

49. In order to bind a contract, what Bible person took off his shoe and gave it to his neighbor?

A: Boaz for Ruth—Ruth 4:7-10

50. What is the name of the five-year-old boy who was dropped by his nurse and became crippled for life?

A: Mephibosheth—2 Samuel 4:4

51. What woman in the Bible gave a man butter and then killed him by driving a nail through his head?

A: Jael—Judges 5:24-26

52. Two lawyers are mentioned in the Bible. What are their names?

A: Gamaliel and Zenas—Acts 5:34; Titus 3:13

53. What is the name of the king who became herbivorous and ate grass like the oxen?

A: King Nebuchadnezzar—Daniel 4:33

54. In what book of the Bible is bad breath mentioned?

A: Job—Job 19:17

55. How long did Noah remain in the Ark?

A: One year and seventeen days (seven days were before it started to rain)—Genesis 7:10,11; 8:13,14

56. Who could use bows and arrows or sling stones with either the right or left hand?

A: David's mighty men—1 Chronicles 12:1,2

57. Who killed a lion in a pit on a snowy day?

A: Benaiah, the son of Jehoiada—1 Chronicles 11:22

58. Who killed 300 men with his own spear?

A: Abishai, brother of Joab—1 Chronicles 11:20

59. What Bible character ate a book and thought it was sweet like honey?

A: Ezekiel—Ezekiel 2:9; 3:3

60. Who was quoted for saying, "Is there any taste in the white of an egg?"

A: Job—Job 6:6

61. During what event in the Bible did dove manure sell for food?

A: During the famine in Samaria—2 Kings 6:25

62. How many different arks are mentioned in the Bible?

A: Three: The Ark of Noah—Genesis 6:14; the ark that Moses slept in—Exodus 2:3; the Ark of the Covenant—Numbers 10:33

63. What Bible character was mentioned as being the first craftsman with brass and iron?

A: Tubal-Cain—Genesis 4:22

64. What is the shortest chapter in the Bible?

A: Psalm 117 (two verses)

65. What is the name of the individual who ate a little book and got indigestion?

A: John the apostle—Revelation 10:10

66. Adam called his helpmate woman and he named her Eve. What did God call Eve?

    A: Adam ("In the day that God created man, in the likeness of God made he him; male and female created he them; and blessed them, and called their name Adam, in the day when they were created")— Genesis 5:1,2

67. What Bible character walked around naked and without shoes for three years?

    A: Isaiah—Isaiah 20:3

68. What is the name of the man who was killed by having a nail driven through his head?

    A: Sisera the Canaanite captain—Judges 4:18-21

69. Who said, "*Eli, Eli, Lama sabachthani*" and what does it mean?

    A: Jesus, and it means "My God, My God, why hast thou forsaken me?"—Matthew 27:46

70. The Bible characters Samson, David, and Benaiah all have one thing in common. What is it?

    A: They all slew a lion—Judges 14:5,6; 1 Samuel 17:34-36; and 2 Samuel 23:20

71. What was the name of the man who killed 800 men with a spear?

    A: Adino the Eznite—2 Samuel 23:8

72. Jesus had how many brothers and sisters?

    A: Four brothers and at least two sisters ("Is not this the carpenter, the son of Mary, the brother of James, and Joses, and of Juda, and Simon? and are not his sisters here with us?")—Mark 6:3

73. Who was the man that killed 600 men with an ox goad?
    A: Shamgar—Judges 3:31

74. What man in the Bible wished that he had been aborted?
    A: Job—Job 3:2,3,11,16

75. The ministering women gave up their brass mirrors to make a bathtub for men to wash in. Who were these men?
    A: Moses, Aaron and his sons—Exodus 38:8; 40:30,31

76. What man in the Bible had hair like eagle feathers and nails like bird claws?
    A: Nebuchadnezzar—Daniel 4:33

77. How many people in the Bible have their name beginning with the letter "Z"?
    A: 188 different people, representing 87 different names, including 27 Zechariahs, 12 Zichris, 9 Zebadiahs, 9 Zadoks, 7 Zabads, 7 Zaccurs, 7 Zerahs, and 5 Zedekiahs

78. What was the name of the king who practiced divination by looking in a liver?
    A: The King of Babylon—Ezekiel 21:21

79. How many men in the Bible are named Dodo?
    A: Three—Judges 10:1; 2 Samuel 23:9; 23:24

80. What was used to join the tabernacle curtains together?
    A: Fifty gold taches (clasps)—Exodus 26:6

81. What was the name of the eight-year-old boy who served as king of Jerusalem for 100 days?
    A: Jehoiachin—2 Chronicles 36:9

82. What man tore his clothes and pulled out his hair because of interracial marriage?
    A: Ezra—Ezra 9:1-3

83. What man tore out other men's hair for interracial marriage?
    A: Nehemiah—Nehemiah 13:23-25

84. Who was the first bigamist to be mentioned in the Bible?
   A: Lamech—Genesis 4:19 (His penalty was two mothers-in-law!)

85. What was the name of the judge in Israel who was a polygamist?
   A: Gideon—Judges 8:30

86. What event caused a donkey's head to be sold for eighty pieces of silver?
   A: The famine in Samaria—2 Kings 6:25

87. In what book of the Bible does it talk about camels wearing necklaces?
   A: Judges—Judges 8:21,26

88. Who fashioned five mice out of gold?
   A: The Philistines—1 Samuel 6:1-5,16,18

89. In what portion of the Bible does it talk about the sole of a dove's foot?
   A: In the story of Noah and the Ark—Genesis 8:9

90. Who was the first drunkard to be talked about in the Bible?
   A: Noah—Genesis 9:20,21

91. In what book in the Bible does it talk about men who neighed after their neighbors' wives?
   A: Jeremiah ("Everyone in Israel neighed after his neighbor's wife")—Jeremiah 5:8

92. In the Old Testament 42,000 were killed for the incorrect pronunciation of one word. What was that word?
   A: Shibboleth—Judges 12:5,6

93. What Bible character shot an arrow through a man's body and who was the man who died?
   A: Jehu shot the arrow and Jehoram died—2 Kings 9:24

94. What is the name of the man who fed seventy kings at his table?

    A: Adonibezek—Judges 1:7

95. Who got so hungry that she ate her own son?

    A: A woman of Samaria during the great famine—2 Kings 6:25,29

96. What was queen Esther's other name?

    A: Hadassah—Esther 2:7

97. There is one place in the Bible where it talks about grease. In what book of the Bible do you find that comment?

    A: Psalms—Psalm 119:70

98. In what book of the Bible does it command brides to shave their heads and manicure their nails?

    A: Deuteronomy—Deuteronomy 21:11,12

99. According to Matthew, who were Joses, Simon, Judas, and James?

    A: The brothers of Jesus—Matthew 13:55

100. Who killed a seven-and-a-half-foot tall Egyptian giant?

    A: Benaiah—1 Chronicles 11:22,23

101. Where is the swimmer's breaststroke mentioned in the Bible?

    A: Isaiah ("As he that swimmeth spreadeth forth his hands to swim")—Isaiah 25:11

102. Twenty-seven-thousand men were killed when a wall of a city fell on them. What was the name of the city where the wall was located?

    A: Aphek—1 Kings 20:30

103. What was the name of the man who killed a giant having twelve fingers and twelve toes?

    A: Jonathan, son of Shimeah—2 Samuel 21:20,21

104. What Bible character burned his son alive as a sacrifice?

A: Ahaz—2 Kings 16:2,3

105. What person in the Bible set fire to 300 foxes' tails?

A: Samson—Judges 15:4

106. What Bible character had neither a father nor mother, is mentioned eleven times in Scripture, was not born and did not die?

A: Melchisedek—Hebrews 7:1-3

107. The book of Proverbs lists four creatures that are small but exceedingly wise. What are these four creatures?

A: Ants, conies (badgers), locusts, and spiders—Proverbs 30:24-28

108. Who warned his enemies by cutting up a yoke of oxen and saying to them that if they did not submit to him, the same thing would happen to them?

A: Saul—1 Samuel 11:7

109. After Jesus had risen from the dead, Peter was fishing and caught a large amount of fish in his net and brought them to Jesus. How many fish did Peter catch in his net?

A: One hundred fifty-three—John 21:11

110. What Bible prophet prophesied that men would eat their own flesh?

A: Isaiah—Isaiah 9:20

111. What person in the Bible said, "A living dog is better than a dead lion"?

A: Solomon—Ecclesiastes 1:1; 9:4

112. Which king set fire to his own palace and died in the flames?

A: Zimri—1 Kings 16:18

113. How many locks of hair did Delilah cut from Samson's hair?

A: Seven—Judges 16:18,19

114. The prophet Ahijah the Shilonite found _____ outside of Jerusalem and tore his new garment into _____ pieces.

A: Jeroboam, twelve pieces—1 Kings 11:29,30

115. What was the name of one of the two friends that met Jesus on the road to Emmaus after the resurrection?

A: Cleopas—Luke 24:13,18

116. The word "ball" is mentioned only one time in the Bible. In what book of the Bible do you find this word?

A: Isaiah—Isaiah 22:18

117. Jerusalem was also known by two other names. What were those names?

A: Jebus—Judges 19:10; Salem—Psalm 76:2

118. How many pieces of silver did the Philistines promise Delilah if she could find out the secret of Samson's strength?

A: Eleven hundred pieces of silver—Judges 16:5

119. Who saw the portraits of handsome young men and fell in love with what she saw?

A: Aholibah—Ezekiel 23:11-16

120. Where do you find the longest verse in the Bible?

A: Esther—Esther 8:7

121. How did Michal, David's wife, help David to escape the king's messengers?

A: She put a dummy in the bed—1 Samuel 19:12-16

122. What prophet talked about a girl being exchanged for a drink (wine)?

A: Joel—Joel 3:3

123. What was the name of the Bible character who had seventy-eight wives and concubines who gave birth to eighty-eight children?

A: Rehoboam—2 Chronicles 11:21

124. There was a certain king who had his women perfumed for a year before they came to him. What was his name?

A: Ahasuerus—Esther 2:12

125. Nahor's two eldest sons were named:
a. Huz and Buz   b. Huz and Muz   c. Buz and Muz
d. Fuz and Suz   e. Huz and Fuz   f. Buz and Suz

A: "A" or Huz and Buz—Genesis 22:20,21

126. Who were the men of whom God said, "Thou shalt make for them girdles, and bonnets"?

A: Aaron's sons—Exodus 28:40

127. Which book in the Bible talks about men who "belch out with their mouth"?

A: Psalms—Psalm 59:7

128. In what book of the Bible does it talk about ice coming out of the womb?

A: Job—Job 38:29

129. Who laughed when threatened with a spear?

A: God—Job 41:29

130. In what book of the Bible do we find mention of "wimples and the crisping pins"?

A: Isaiah—Isaiah 3:22

131. What is the name of the Bible character who had 30 sons who rode on 30 donkeys and controlled 30 cities?

A: Jair—Judges 10:3,4

132. In what book of the Bible do we have the first mention of a barber's razor?

A: Numbers—Numbers 6:5

133. The angel of the Lord killed how many of Sennach-erib's soldiers?

A: One hundred eighty-five thousand—Isaiah 37:36,37

134. How many times is the Old Testament quoted in the book of Revelation?

A: Two hundred and forty-five

135. In what verse of the Bible do we find the word "canker-worm" mentioned twice?

A: Nahum 3:15

136. In what book of the Bible do we find the only two occurrences of the word rainbow?

A: Revelation—Revelation 4:3; 10:1

137. In what book of the Bible do we read the words, "Twisting the nose produces blood" (NIV)?

A: Proverbs—Proverbs 30:33

138. What is the name of the Bible character who said, "I have escaped with only the skin of my teeth" (NIV)?

A: Job—Job 19:20

139. According to King Solomon, good news gives health to what part of our body?

A: Bones—Proverbs 15:30

140. How long did Ezekiel lie on his right side for the sins of Judah?

A: Forty days—Ezekiel 4:6

141. What book of the Bible talks about "five gold tumors and five gold rats" (NIV)?

A: 1 Samuel—1 Samuel 6:4

142. The bronze snake that Moses made was broken into pieces by what king?

A: Hezekiah—2 Kings 18:1-4

143. What Bible character was smothered to death by a wet cloth?

    A: Ben-Hadad (NIV)—2 Kings 8:14,15

144. Which chapter in the book of Psalms could be a statement against abortion?

    A: Psalm 139—Psalm 139:13-16

145. What book of the Bible talks about a man "that hath a flat nose"?

    A: Leviticus—Leviticus 21:18

146. What Bible character was known for his threats to gouge out the right eye of the people who lived in Jabesh Gilead?

    A: Nahash—1 Samuel 11:1,2

147. How close to the city of Jericho was the brook of Ziba?

    A: Not close at all. Ziba was one of King Saul's servants—2 Samuel 9:2

148. Who was the high priest when Nehemiah rebuilt the walls of Jerusalem?

    A: Eliashib—Nehemiah 3:1

149. How many men did Solomon use to cut stone for the temple?

    A: Eighty thousand (NIV)—1 Kings 5:15-17

150. The Bible says that what bird is cruel to her young?

    A: Ostrich—Job 39:13-17

151. God spoke to Jeremiah and said something that is a good argument against abortion. What was that statement?

    A: "Before I formed you in the womb, I knew you" (NIV)—Jeremiah 1:5

152. What was the name of Ezekiel's father?

    A: Buzi—Ezekiel 1:3

153. What Bible character thought laughter was a foolish thing?

A: Solomon—Ecclesiastes 2:2

154. In what book of the Bible do you find the first mention of using battering rams against gates of a city?

A: Ezekiel 21:22

155. God showed a basket to the prophet Amos. What was in that basket?

A: Fruit—Amos 8:1

156. The word eternity is used _____ times in the Bible.

A: Once—Isaiah 57:15

157. Ahab's 70 sons had their heads cut off and sent in baskets to what man?

A: Jehu—2 Kings 10:1-7

158. Which Bible character had the first king-sized bed?

A: Og, king of Basham—Deuteronomy 3:11

159. In which two books of the Bible do we read about cannibalism?

A: 2 Kings and Lamentations—2 Kings 6:28,29; Lamentations 4:10

160. Which family in the Bible did not have to pay taxes?

A: Jesse's family—1 Samuel 17:17,25,50

161. The Bible says that storks build their nests in what kind of trees?

A: Pine (NIV); fir (KJV)—Psalm 104:17

162. How did God destroy the kings who attacked Gibeon?

A: With hailstones—Joshua 10:5,11

163. In what book of the Bible does it talk about nose jewelry?

A: Isaiah—Isaiah 3:21

164. What Bible character had this thumbs and big toes cut off by the tribes of Judah and Simeon?
A: Adoni-Bezek—Judges 1:3-6

165. What Bible character hid his belt (girdle—KJV) in the crevice of the rocks?
A: Jeremiah—Jeremiah 13:3-5

166. What is the name of the young virgin who kept King David warm during his old age?
A: Abishag—1 Kings 1:1-3

167. King Saul sat under what kind of tree while Jonathan went to attack the Philistines?
A: A pomegranate tree—1 Samuel 14:1,2

168. What was the name of Abraham's servant?
A: Eliezer of Damascus—Genesis 15:2,3

169. How many chapters are there in the entire Bible?
A: 1189

170. Who was the father of Ziddim, Zer, Hammath, Rakkath, and Kinnereth?
A: No one. They were fortified cities—Joshua 19:35

171. How many chapters are there in the Old Testament?
A: 929

172. What Bible character was beheaded, cremated, and then buried?
A: King Saul—1 Samuel 31:8-13

173. In what book of the Bible do we find mention of "mufflers"?
A: Isaiah—Isaiah 3:19

174. Gideon received golden earrings as payment for conquering the Midianites. How much did the earrings weigh?
A: The same as 1700 shekels of gold—Judges 8:26

175. What is the most used word in the Bible?
   A: "The"

176. The valley of Siddim was famous for what?
   A: Tar pits (NIV); slimepits (KJV)—Genesis 14:10

177. Where was Ishbosheth's head buried?
   A: In Abner's tomb at Hebron—2 Samuel 4:12

178. When the tabernacle was built, who was the chief craftsman?
   A: Bezalel—Exodus 31:1-5

179. What emotion will cause your bones to rot?
   A: Envy—Proverbs 14:30

180. What group of people were told to burn their hair after it was cut off?
   A: The Nazarites—Numbers 6:18

181. Who was told to say, "My little finger is thicker than my father's waist" (NIV)?
   A: Rehoboam—2 Chronicles 10:6,7,10

182. In what book of the Bible do you find the "hill of the foreskins"?
   A: Joshua—Joshua 5:3

183. Hezekiah had a poultice put on his boil. What was the poultice made of?
   A: Figs—2 Kings 20:7

184. What was the name of Goliath's brother?
   A: Lahmi—1 Chronicles 20:5

185. What three things did the Pharisees and scribes tithe?
   A: Mint, dill (anise—KJV), cummin—Matthew 23:23

186. What are the names of the two women who had their ages recorded in the Bible?
   A: Sarah and Anna—Genesis 23:1; Luke 2:36,37

187. What was the name of the eunuch who was in charge of King Xerxes' (King Ahasuerus—KJV) concubines?

A: Shaashgaz—Esther 2:12-14

188. What Bible character is mentioned as having an incurable bowel disease?

A: Jehoram—2 Chronicles 21:18

189. What Bible character said that soldiers should be content with their pay?

A: John the Baptist—Luke 3:14,15

190. The horses of the Babylonians (Chaldeans—KJV) were likened to what kind of animals?

a. Lions   b. Leopards c. Deer   d. Sheep
e. Eagles

A: "B" or leopards—Habakkuk 1:6-8

191. What did Moses throw into the air to signal the start of the plague of boils on Egypt?

A: Soot (NIV); ashes (KJV)—Exodus 9:8-10

192. In what book of the Bible do we find mention of "round tires like the moon"?

A: Isaiah—Isaiah 3:18

193. In Zechariah's vision, the man on the red horse was riding among what kind of trees?

A: Myrtle—Zechariah 1:8

194. What is the name of the man who tried to humiliate David's army by cutting off half of each soldier's beard and their garments in the middle at the buttocks?

A: Hanun the Ammonite—2 Samuel 10:4

195. What is the name of the man who wrote Proverbs 30?

A: Agur—Proverbs 30:1

196. In the book of Revelation, Antipas was martyred in
_____ for his faith.

A: Pergamum—Revelation 2:12,13

197. How many Bible characters are mentioned as living
over 900 years?

a. 3   b. 5   c. 7   d. 9   e. 11

A: "C' or 7—Genesis 5:5,8,11,14,20,27; 9:29

198. Solomon made the steps of the temple and the palace
out of what kind of wood?

A: Algum wood (NIV)—2 Chronicles 9:10,11

199. What were the first words Elisha spoke when he saw
Elijah going to heaven?

A: "My, father, my father"—2 Kings 2:11,12

200. How many suicides are mentioned in the Bible?

A: Seven

201. The wicked King Abimelech was critically injured by a
woman dropping a _____ on his head.

A: Millstone—Judges 9:53

202. How many days was Ezekiel told to lie on his side while
eating only bread and water?

A: Three hundred and ninety—Ezekiel 4:9-11

203. King Asa had what kind of disease?

A: A foot disease—2 Chronicles 16:12

204. God punished David for taking a census of the people.
How many people died in God's punishment?

A: Seventy thousand—1 Chronicles 21:1,14

205. The Israelites were told not to destroy what when they
besieged cities in the Old Testament?

A: The trees—Deuteronomy 20:19

206. How many shekels of silver did Achan steal?

A: Two hundred—Joshua 7:20,21

207. The name Judas Iscariot appears how many times in
     the Bible?
     A: Ten

208. When Rachel stole some household gods from her
     father, she hid them in a camel's saddle and sat on the
     saddle. When her father came looking for the images,
     what excuse did Rachel use for not getting off the
     camel's saddle?
     A: She was having her period—Genesis 31:34,35

209. Obadiah hid _____ prophets in caves to protect them
     from Jezebel?
     A: One hundred—1 Kings 18:4

210. When the tower of Siloam fell, how many people were
     killed?
     A: Eighteen—Luke 13:4

211. What Bible character talks about beautiful feet?
     A: Isaiah—Isaiah 52:7

212. In what book of the Bible does it say, "Our skin was
     black like an oven because of the terrible famine"?
     A: Lamentations—Lamentations 5:10

213. In what book of the Bible do we find the famous verse,
     "At Parbar westward, four at the causeway, and two at
     Parbar"?
     A: 1 Chronicles—1 Chronicles 26:18

214. What Bible character cooked his bread on cow dung?
     A: Ezekiel—Ezekiel 4:15

215. Name the only book in the Bible that is addressed
     specifically to a woman.
     A: 2 John—2 John 1

216. How many people were shipwrecked with the apostle
     Paul in the book of Acts?
     A: Two hundred seventy six—Acts 27:37,41

217. Who was the famous father of Maher-Shalel-Hash-Baz?

A: Isaiah—Isaiah 8:3

218. What is the name of the king of Judah who made war machines that could shoot arrows and hurl huge stones?

A: Uzziah—2 Chronicles 26:11,15

219. What was the name of Haman's wife?

A: Zeresh—Esther 5:10,11

220. How many times does the name Satan appear in the Bible?

A: Fifty-three

221. The manna in the wilderness was likened to what kind of seed?

A: Coriander—Numbers 11:7

222. What will bring "health to thy navel and marrow to thy bones"?

A: Fearing the Lord and departing from evil—Proverbs 3:7,8

223. Which town in the Bible had silver heaped up like dust and fine gold like the dirt of the streets?

A: Tyre (NIV); Tyrus (KJV)—Zechariah 9:3

224. In what book of the Bible do we have mention of "sea monsters"?

A: Lamentations—Lamentations 4:3

225. How many times is the word Lord mentioned in the Bible?

a. 5,017   b. 6,370   c. 7,736   d. 8,212   e. 9,108

A: "C" or 7,736

226. In what two books of the Bible does it talk about men drinking their own urine and eating their own refuse?

A: 2 Kings and Isaiah—2 Kings 18:27; Isaiah 36:12

227. Which book of the Bible mentions men "fearing lest they should fall into the quicksands"?
A: Acts—Acts 27:17

228. To whom did Ebed-melech, the Ethiopian say, "Put now these... rotten rags under thine armholes"?
A: Jeremiah—Jeremiah 38:12

229. What man in the Bible did not shave or wash his clothes for many days?
A: Mephibosheth—2 Samuel 19:24

230. Who grabbed Amasa by the beard with his right hand and pretended that he was going to kiss him, but instead stabbed him with a dagger?
A: Joab—2 Samuel 20:9,10

231. How many times is Beer mentioned in the Bible?
A: twice—Numbers 21:16; Judges 9:21

232. In what book of the Bible do we have the only mention of a ferry boat?
A: 2 Samuel—2 Samuel 19:18

233. What two tribes built an altar between them and called it Ed?
A: Reuben and Gad—Joshua 22:34

234. Where in the Bible does it talk about a gathering of the sheriffs?
A: Daniel—Daniel 3:2

235. In which book of the Bible does it talk about melting slugs or snails?
A: Psalms—Psalm 58:8

236. How many times is the word "the" used in the Bible?
a. Over 9,000   b. Over 11,000   c. Over 14,000
d. Over 20,000
A: "D" or over 20,000 times

237. In what book of the Bible do we find mention of stars singing?

A: Job—Job 38:7

238. How many times is the word suburbs mentioned in the Bible?

A: One hundred and fifteen

239. How many times are unicorns mentioned in the Bible?

A: Nine—Numbers 23:22; 24:8; Deuteronomy 33:17; Job 39:9,10; Psalm 22:21; 29:6; 92:10; Isaiah 34:7

240. Who was the brother of Zered?

A: No one. Zered was a valley (NIV) or brook (KJV)—Deuteronomy 2:13

241. If Cain was avenged sevenfold, how many times would Lamech be avenged?

A: Seventy-seven—Genesis 4:24

242. To how many people did God say, "Be fruitful, and multiply, and replenish the earth"?

A: Six—Adam, Eve, Noah, Shem, Ham, and Japheth—Genesis 1:28; 9:1

243. What time of day did God rain down fire and brimstone on Sodom and Gomorrah?

A: Early in the morning—Genesis 19:23,24

244. What did Abraham call the name of the place where he was about to sacrifice Isaac?

A: Jehovah-jireh, "the Lord will provide"—Genesis 22:14

245. How old was Esau when he married his two wives Judith and Basemath?

A: Forty—Genesis 26:34

246. Isaiah prophesied that _____ women would take hold of one man.

A: Seven—Isaiah 4:1

247. Zechariah saw a vision of a scroll that was _____ feet long.

A: Thirty (twenty cubits)—Zechariah 5:1,2

248. Who was the first man to say, "I have sinned" in the Bible?

A: Pharaoh—Exodus 9:27

249. The Bible character Zaphenath-Paneah was known by another famous name. What was that name?

A: Joseph, son of Jacob—Genesis 41:45

250. In Zechariah's vision, the flying scroll was how wide?

A: Fifteen feet (ten cubits)—Zechariah 5:1,2

ANSWERS TO PUNS RIDDLES, AND HUMOROUS TRIVIA QUESTIONS

1. What was the name of Isaiah's horse?
   A: Is Me. Isaiah said, "Woe is me."

2. Who was the first man in the Bible to know the meaning of rib roast?
   A: Adam

3. Where does it talk about Honda cars in the Bible?
   A: In Acts 1:14—"These all continued with one *accord*."

4. Who is the smallest man in the Bible?
   A: Some people believe that it was Zacchaeus. Others believe it was Nehemiah (Ne-high-a-miah), or Bildad, the Shuhite (Shoe-height). But in reality it was Peter the disciple. He slept on his watch!

5. Where in the Bible does it say that we should not play marbles?
   A: In John 3:7—Jesus said to Nicodemus, "Marvel not..." (Marble-Not)

6. How were Adam and Eve prevented from gambling?
   A: Their paradise (pair-o-dice) was taken away from them.

7. Where does it say in the Bible that we should not fly in airplanes?
   A: In Matthew 28:20—"Lo (Low), I am with you always" ...not high up in the air.

8. What did Noah say while he was loading all the animals on the Ark?

   A: "Now I herd everything."

9. When did Moses sleep with five people in one bed?

   A: When he slept with his forefathers.

10. Where in the Bible does it talk about smoking?

    A: In Genesis 24:64—Rebekah lighted off her camel.

11. What was the first theatrical event in the Bible?

    A: Eve's appearance for Adam's benefit

12. Where in the Bible does it say that fathers should let their sons use the automobile?

    A: In Proverbs 13:24—"He that spareth his rod hateth his son."

13. Why are there so few men with whiskers in heaven?

    A: Because most men get in by a close shave.

14. Who was the best financier in the Bible?

    A: Noah. He floated his stock while the whole world was in liquidation.

15. What simple affliction brought about the death of Samson?

    A: Fallen arches

16. What did Adam and Eve do when they were expelled from the Garden of Eden?

    A: They raised Cain.

17. What are two of the smallest insects mentioned in the Bible?

    A: The widow's "mite," and the "wicked flee"—Mark 12:24 and Proverbs 28:1

18. In what place did the cock crow when all the world could hear him?

    A: On Noah's Ark

19. What were the Phoenicians famous for?
    A: Blinds

20. Where was deviled ham mentioned in the Bible?
    A: When the evil spirits entered the swine.

21. Who introduced the first walking stick?
    A: Eve...when she presented Adam a little Cain.

22. Where is medicine first mentioned in the Bible?
    A: Where the Lord gives Moses two tablets.

23. Where in the Bible does it suggest that men should wash dishes?
    A: In 2 Kings 21:13—"And I will wipe Jerusalem as a man wipeth a dish, wiping it, and turning it upside down."

24. Where did Noah strike the first nail in the Ark?
    A: On the head

25. Why was Moses the most wicked man in the Bible?
    A: Because he broke the Ten Commandments all at once.

26. What man in the Bible spoke when he was a very small baby?
    A: Job. He cursed the day he was born.

27. At what time of day was Adam born?
    A: A little before Eve

28. What man in the Bible had no parents?
    A: Joshua, the son of Nun

29. Where is tennis mentioned in the Bible?
    A: When Joseph served in Pharaoh's court

30. Was there any money on Noah's Ark?
    A: Yes, The duck took a bill, the frog took a greenback, and the skunk took a scent.

31. Paul the apostle was a great preacher and teacher and earned his living as a tentmaker. What other occupation did Paul have?

    A: He was a baker. We know this because he went to Philippi (Fill-a-pie).

32. Why was Adam's first day the longest?

    A: Because it had no Eve.

33. Why was the woman in the Bible turned into a pillar of salt?

    A: Because she was dissatisfied with her Lot.

34. What is the story in the Bible that talks about a very lazy man?

    A: The story about the fellow that loafs and fishes

35. Why didn't the last dove return to the Ark?

    A: Because she had sufficient grounds to stay away.

36. Who was the most successful physician in the Bible?

    A: Job. He had the most patience (patients).

37. How do we know they used arithmetic in early Bible times?

    A: Because the Lord said to multiply on the face of the earth.

38. How long a period of time did Cain hate his brother?

    A: As long as he was Abel

39. Who was the first electrician in the Bible?

    A: Noah, when he took his family and the animals out of the Ark it made the Ark light (arclight).

40. Who sounded the first bell in the Bible?

    A: Cain when he hit Abel

41. How did Jonah feel when the great fish swallowed him?

    A: Down in the mouth

42. Why are a pair of roller skates like the forbidden fruit in the Garden of Eden?

    A: They both come before the fall.

43. What does the story of Jonah and the great fish teach us?

    A: You can't keep a good man down.

44. Do you know how you can tell that David was older than Goliath?

    A: Because David rocked Goliath to sleep.

45. What is the difference between Noah's Ark and an archbishop?

    A: One was a high ark, but the other is a hierarch

46. When did Ruth treat Boaz badly?

    A: When she pulled his ears and trod on his corn

47. Where was Solomon's temple located?

    A: On the side of his head

48. Who is the fastest runner in the world?

    A: Adam, because he was first in the human race.

49. If Moses were alive today, why would he be considered a remarkable man?

    A: Because he would be several thousand years old.

50. How do we know that Noah had a pig in the Ark?

    A: He had Ham.

51. Why did Moses cross the Red Sea?

    A: To avoid Egyptian traffic

52. Who was the most popular actor in the Bible?

    A: Samson. He brought the house down.

53. Who was the most ambitious man in the Bible?

    A: Jonah, because even the great fish couldn't keep him down

54. Who were the twin boys in the Bible?

    A: First and Second Samuel

55. Where is baseball mentioned in the Bible?

    A: Genesis 1:1—In the Beginning (big inning)
    Genesis 3:6—Eve stole first and Adam stole second
    Genesis 24:15,16—Rebekah went to the well with a
       "pitcher"
    Luke 15:11-32—The prodigal son made a home run
    Judges—When Gideon rattled the pitchers
    Exodus 4:4—"And he put forth his hand, and caught it"
    Numbers 11:32—"ten homers"
    Psalm 19:12—Who can understand my errors?
    Proverbs 18:10—"The righteous runneth into it, and is
       safe"
    Ezekiel 36:12—"Yea, I will cause men to walk"

56. Who was the first person in the Bible to eat herself out of
    house and home?

    A: Eve

57. Why was Job always cold in bed?

    A: Because he had such miserable comforters.

58. How were the Egyptians paid for good taken by the
    Israelites when they fled from Egypt?

    A: The Egyptians got a check on the bank of the Red
       Sea.

59. Why didn't they play cards on Noah's Ark?

    A: Because Noah sat on the deck.

60. In the story of the Good Samaritan, why did the Levite
    pass by on the other side?

    A: Because the poor man had already been robbed.

61. Who was the straightest man in the Bible?

    A: Joseph. Pharaoh made a ruler out of him.

62. Which came first—the chicken or the egg?

A: The chicken, of course. God doesn't lay any eggs.

63. When is high finance first mentioned in the Bible?

A: When Pharaoh's daughter took a little prophet (profit) from the bulrushes

64. What is the only wage that does not have any deductions?

A: The wages of sin

65. At what season of the year did Eve eat the fruit?

A: Early in the fall

66. If Methuselah was the oldest man in the Bible (969 years of age), why did he die before his father?

A: His father was Enoch. Enoch never died, he was translated.

67. What has God never seen, Abraham Lincoln seldom saw, and we see every day?

A: Isaiah 40:25; 46:5—" 'To whom then will ye liken me, or shall I be equal?' saith the Holy One." God has never seen his equal, Abraham Lincoln seldom saw his equal, and we see our equals every day.

68. On the Ark, Noah probably got milk from the cows. What did he get from the ducks?

A: Quackers

69. One of the first things Cain did after he left the Garden of Eden was to take a nap. How do we know this?

A: Because he went to the land of Nod—Genesis 4:16.

70. Where do you think the Israelites may have deposited their money?

A: At the banks of the Jordan

71. Why do you think that the kangaroo was the most miserable animal on the Ark?

    A: Because her children had to play inside during the rain.

72. What prophet in the Bible was a space traveler?

    A: Elijah. He went up in a fiery chariot—2 Kings 2:11.

73. What do you have that Cain, Abel, and Seth never had?

    A: Grandparents

74. What city in the Bible was named after something that you find on every modern-day car?

    A: Tyre (tire)

75. When the Ark landed on Mount Ararat, was Noah the first one out?

    A: No, he came fourth out of the Ark.

76. What was the difference between the 10,000 soldiers of Israel and the 300 soldiers Gideon chose for battle?

    A: 9700

77. Where is the first math problem mentioned in the Bible?

    A: When God divided the light from the darkness

78. Where is the second math problem mentioned in the Bible?

    A: When God told Adam and Eve to go forth and multiply—Genesis 1:28.

79. Why did Noah have to punish and discipline the chickens on the Ark?

    A: Because they were using "fowl" language.

80. What was the most expensive meal served in the Bible and who ate it?

    A: Esau. It cost him his birthright—Genesis 25:34.

81. Certain days in the Bible passed by more quickly that
    most of the days. Which days were these?
    A: The fast days

82. Matthew and Mark have something that is not found in
    Luke and John. What is it?
    A: The letter "a"

83. Which one of Noah's sons was considered to be a clown?
    A: His second son. He was always a Ham.

84. What was the first game mentioned in the Bible?
    A: When Adam and Eve played hide-and-seek with God

85. What made Abraham so smart?
    A: He knew a Lot.

86. What is most of the time black, sometimes brown or
    white, but should be red?
    A: The Bible

87. Why did everyone on the Ark think that the horses were
    pessimistic?
    A: Because they always said neigh.

88. Who was the first person in the Bible to have surgery
    performed on him?
    A: Adam, when God removed one of his ribs—Genesis
       2:21.

89. When was the Red Sea very angry?
    A: When the children of Israel crossed it

90. What vegetable did Noah not want on the Ark?
    A: Leeks

91. Why do you think Jonah could not trust the ocean?
    A: He knew that there was something fishy in it.

92. How do we know that God has a sense of humor?
    A: Because He can take a "rib."

93. What time was it when the hippopotamus sat on Noah's rocking chair?

    A: Time to get a new chair

94. What does God both give away and keep at the same time?

    A: His promises

95. During the six days of creation, which weighed more—the day or the night?

    A: The night, because the day was light

96. What did the skunks on the Ark have that no other animals had?

    A: Baby skunks

97. What type of tea does the Bible suggest that we not drink?

    A: Vanity (vani-tea)

98. In what book of the Bible do we find something that is in modern-day courtrooms?

    A: Judges

99. Which animal on the Ark was the rudest?

    A: The mockingbird

100. What kind of soap did God use to keep the oceans clean?

    A: Tide

101. How do we know that the disciples were very cruel to the corn?

    A: Because they pulled its ears.

102. Why did the rooster refuse to fight on the Ark?

    A: Because he was chicken.

103. Why didn't Cain please the Lord with his offering?

    A: He simply wasn't Abel.

104. One of the names of the books of the Bible contains an insect in it. Which one is it?

    A: Ti-(moth)-y

105. How many animals could Noah put into the empty Ark?

    A: One. After that the Ark would not be empty.

106. Which man in the Bible might have only been 12 inches?

    A: Nicodemus, because he was a ruler—John 3:1

107. Which book in the Bible is the counting book?

    A: Numbers

108. What kind of lights did Noah have on the Ark?

    A: Flood lights

109. Gideon had 70 sons. How many of them were big men when they were born?

    A: None of them. They were all babies.

110. Which candle burns longer—the candle hidden under a bushel or the candle set on a hill?

    A: Neither one. They both burn shorter.

111. Which animal on Noah's Ark had the highest level of intelligence?

    A: The giraffe

112. What indication is there that there may have been newspaper reporters in the New Testament?

    A: Because Zacchaeus couldn't see Jesus "for the press"—Luke 19:3

113. The name of one book of the Bible contains an ugly old woman. Which book is it?

    A: (Hag)-gai

114. Which animal on the Ark did Noah not trust?

    A: The cheetah

115. Which Bible character was as strong as steel?
    A: Iron—Joshua 19:38

116. What man in the Bible is named after a chicken?
    A: Hen—Zechariah 6:14

117. Where does the Bible suggest that it is okay to be
    overweight?
    A: Leviticus 3:16—"All the fat is the Lord's."

118. What Bible character had a name that rang a bell?
    A: Mehetable (Ma-hit-a-bell)—Nehemiah 6:10

119. Which bird on Noah's Ark was a thief?
    A: A robin

120. Where does the Bible suggest that newspapers, maga-
    zines, radio, and television are powerful?
    A: Esther 1:3—"The power of Persia and Media...."

121. What is the name of the individual who was perfect in
    the Bible?
    A: Mark—Psalm 37:37: "Mark the perfect man, and
    behold the upright."

122. What was Eve's formal name?
    A: Madam Adam

123. On Noah's Ark, why did the dog have so many friends?
    A: Because he wagged his tail instead of his tongue.

124. Who killed a fourth of all the people in the world?
    A: Cain when he killed Abel—Genesis 4:1,2,8

125. Where does it suggest that there may have been buses
    in the Bible?
    A: In Proverbs 30:31 where it talks about the grey-
    hound.

126. When Eve left the garden without Adam, what did Adam say?

A: Eve is absent without leaf.

127. When a camel with no hump was born on the Ark, what did Noah name it?

A: Humphrey

128. How long did Samson love Delilah?

A: Until she bald him out.

129. Where were freeways first mentioned in the Bible?

A: Genesis 1:30—"The Lord made every creeping thing."

130. What is the name of the sleepiest land in the Bible?

A: The land of Nod—Genesis 4:16

131. What did Noah call the cat that fell into the pickle barrel on the Ark?

A: A sour puss

132. What age were the goats when Adam named them in the Garden of Eden?

A: They were only kids.

133. David played a dishonest musical instrument. What was it called?

A: The lyre

134. Which of the Old Testament prophets were blind?

A: Ezra, Hosea, Joel, Amos, Jonah, Nahum, Habakkuk. None of them have i's.

135. How did Noah keep the milk from turning sour on the ark?

A: He left it in the cow.

136. How many books in the Old Testament were named after Esther?

A: Twenty-two. The rest were named before Esther.

137. What would have happened if all the women would have left the nation of Israel?

    A: It would be have been a stagnation.

138. Why did the giant fish finally let Jonah go?

    A: He couldn't stomach him.

139. Why was Moses buried in a valley in the land of Moab near Bethpeor?

    A: Because he was dead.

140. The name of a book of the Bible contains a fruit. Which book is it?

    A: Phi-(lemon)

141. What is in the wall of Jerusalem that the Israelites did not put there?

    A: Cracks

142. Why was the "W" the nastiest letter in the Bible?

    A: Because it always makes ill will

143. How did Joseph learn to tell the naked truth?

    A: By exposing the bare facts.

144. What food did Samson eat to become strong?

    A: Mussels

145. Why did the tower of Babel stand in the land of Shinar?

    A: Because it couldn't sit down.

146. Why did Moses have to be hidden quickly when he was a baby?

    A: Saving him was a rush job.

147. Where in the Bible do we find the authority for women to kiss men?

    A: Matthew 7:12—"Whatsoever ye would that men should do to you, do ye even so to them."

148. What two things could Samson the Nazarite never eat for breakfast?

A: Lunch and supper

149. If Elijah was invited to dinner and was served only a beet, what would he say?

A: That beet's all.

150. If a man crosses the Sea of Galilee twice without a bath, what would he be?

A: A dirty double-crosser

151. If someone wanted to be converted by John the Baptist, what was the first requirement?

A: You had to go from bad to immerse.

152. What day of the week was the best for cooking manna in the wilderness?

A: Friday

153. If a soft answer turneth away wrath, what does a hard answer do?

A: It turneth wrath your way.

154. In what book of the Bible does it talk about people wearing tires on their heads?

A: Ezekiel—Ezekiel 24:23

155. What is the golden rule of the animal world?

A: Do unto otters as you would have them do unto you.

156. How did Adam and Eve feel when they left the garden?

A: A little put out.

157. Samson was a very strong man but there was one thing he could not hold for very long. What was that?

A: His breath

158. If Moses would have dropped his rod in the Red Sea, what would it have become?

A: Wet

159. What fur did Adam and Eve wear?

A: Bareskin

160. Why must Elijah's parents have been good business people?

A: Because they made a prophet

161. Jesus and the giant fish that swallowed Jonah have something in common. What is it?

A: Jesus had dinner with a sinner and the giant fish had a sinner for dinner.

162. What did Joseph in the Old Testament have in common with Zaccheus in the New Testament?

A: Joseph's job was overseeing, and Zaccheus' problem was seeing over.

163. In what way does an attorney resemble a rabbi?

A: The attorney studies the law and the profits.

164. What does a Christian man love more than life;
Have more than death or mortal strife;
That which contented men desire;
The poor have, the rich require;
The miser spends, the spendthrift saves;
And all men carry to their graves?

A: Nothing

165. What is that which Adam never saw or possessed, yet left two for each of his children?

A: Parents

166. What is greater than God, not as wicked as Satan, if people are alive and eat it they will die, and dead people eat it?

A: Nothing